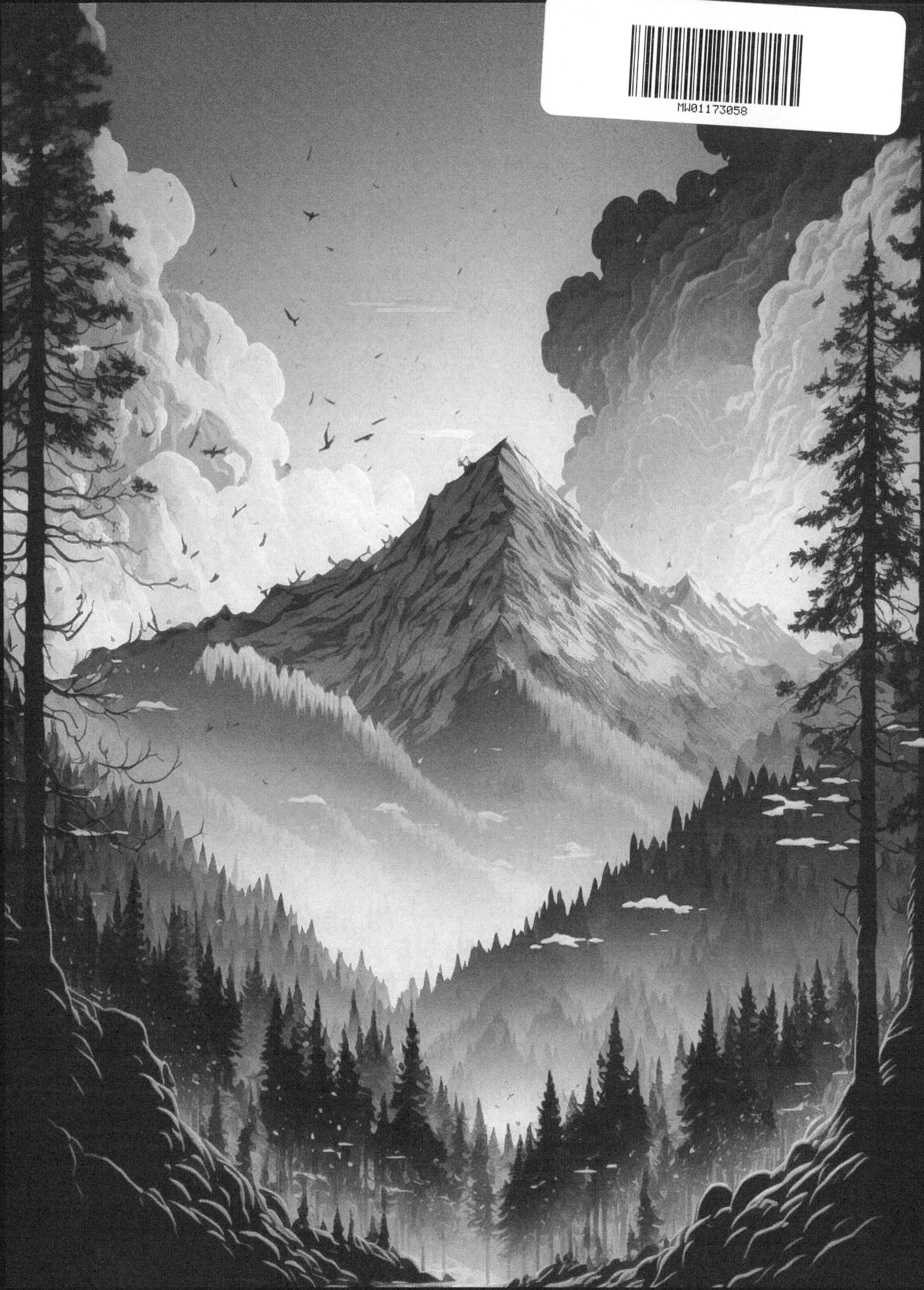

THIS COLORING BOOK BELONGS TO

____

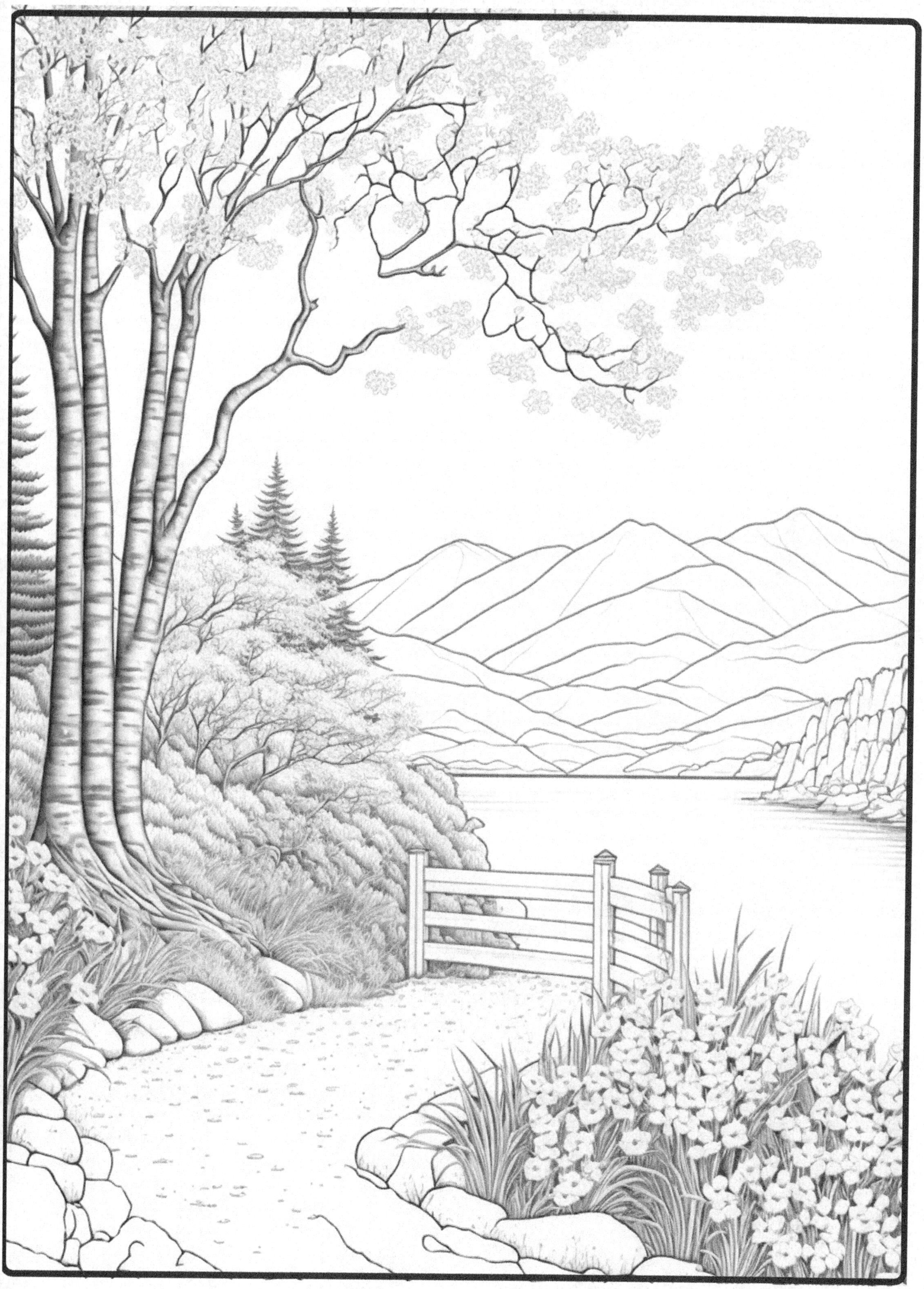

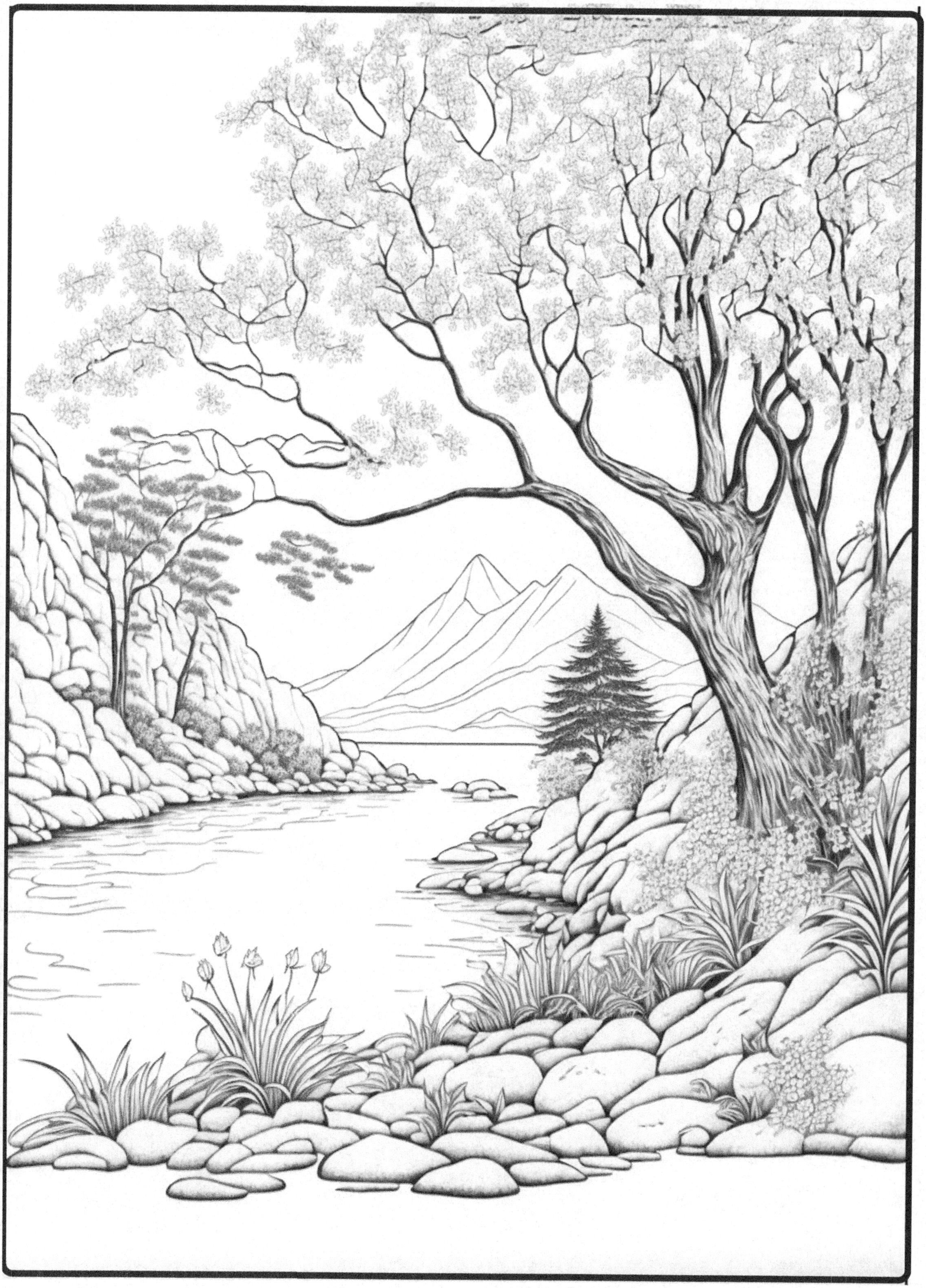

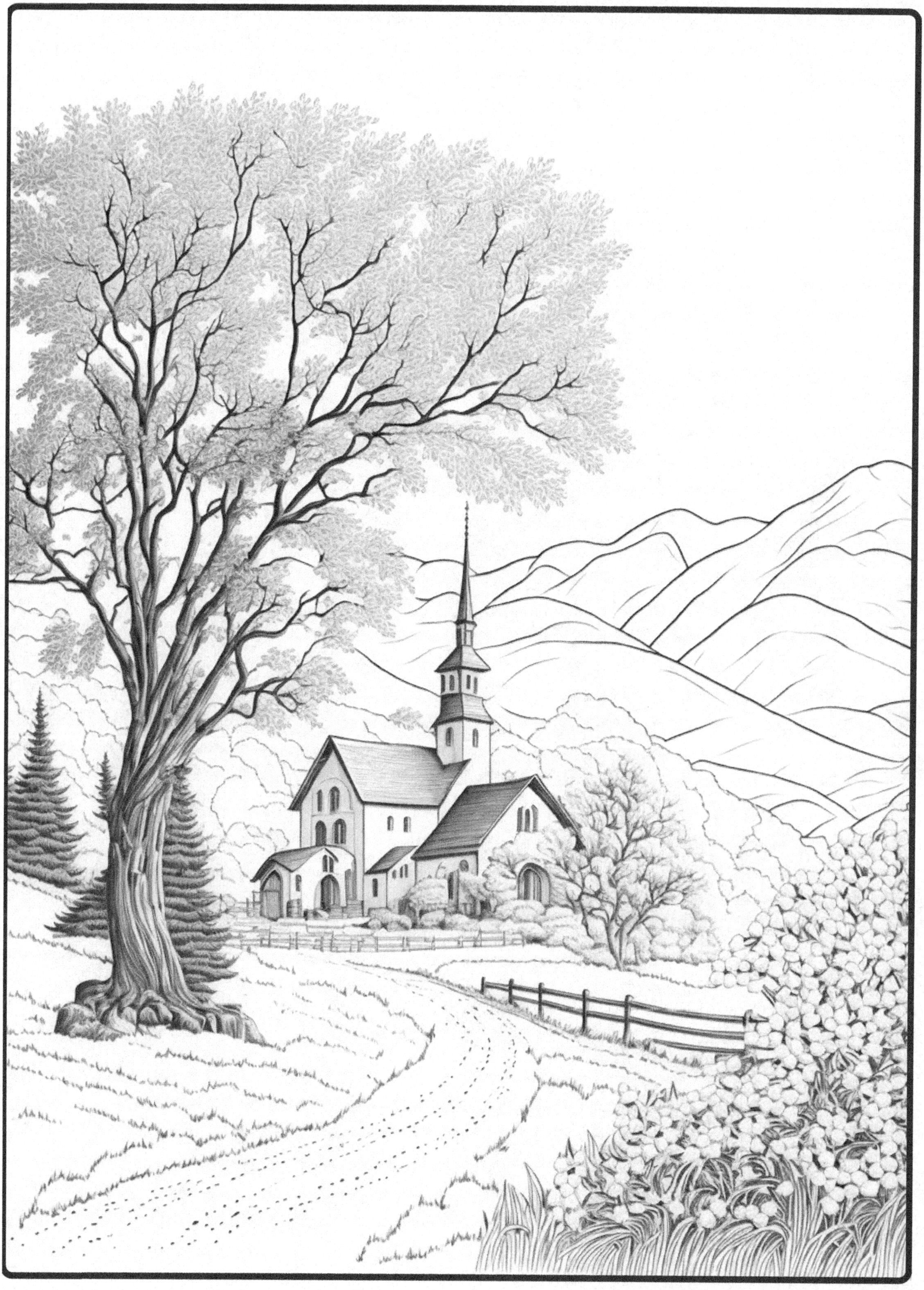

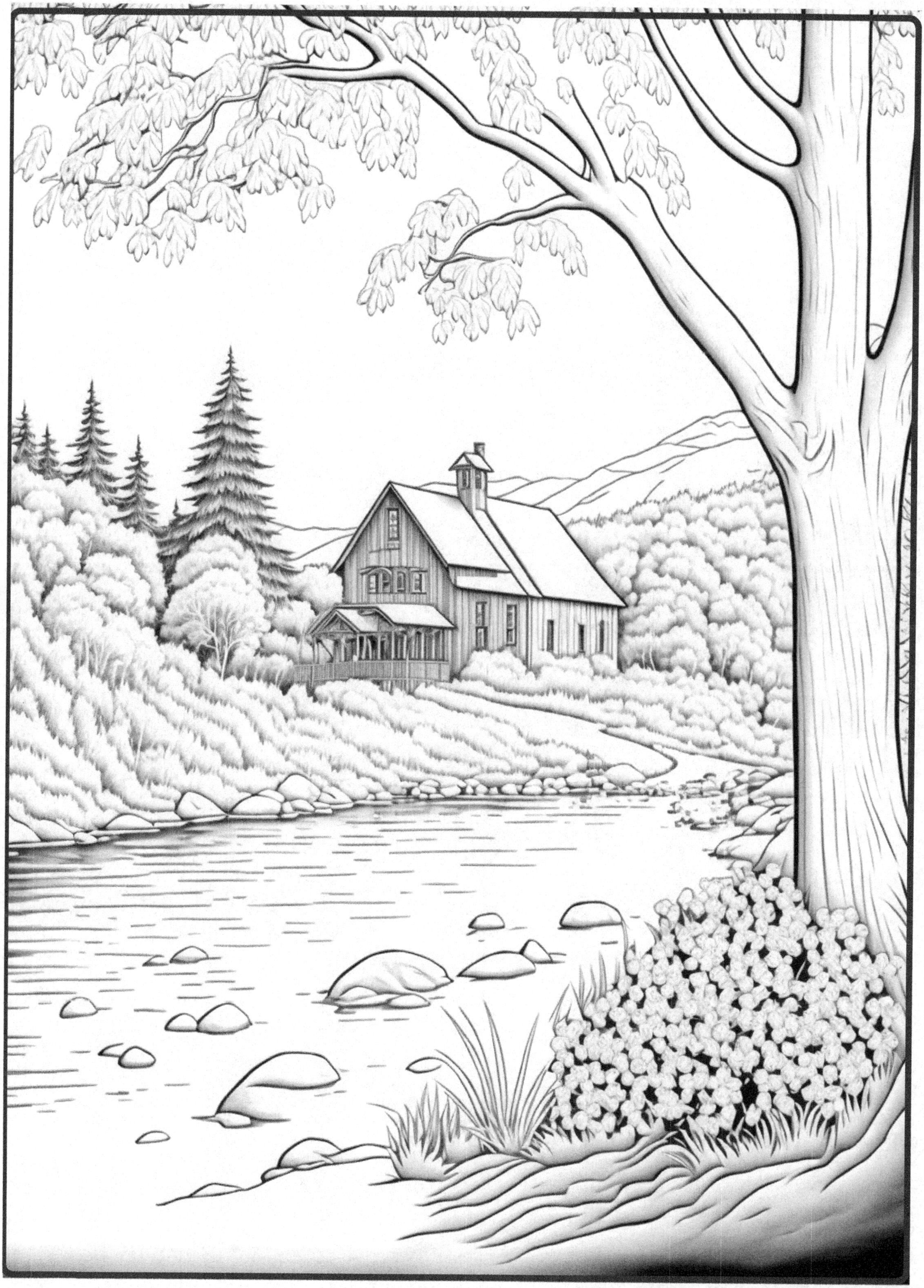

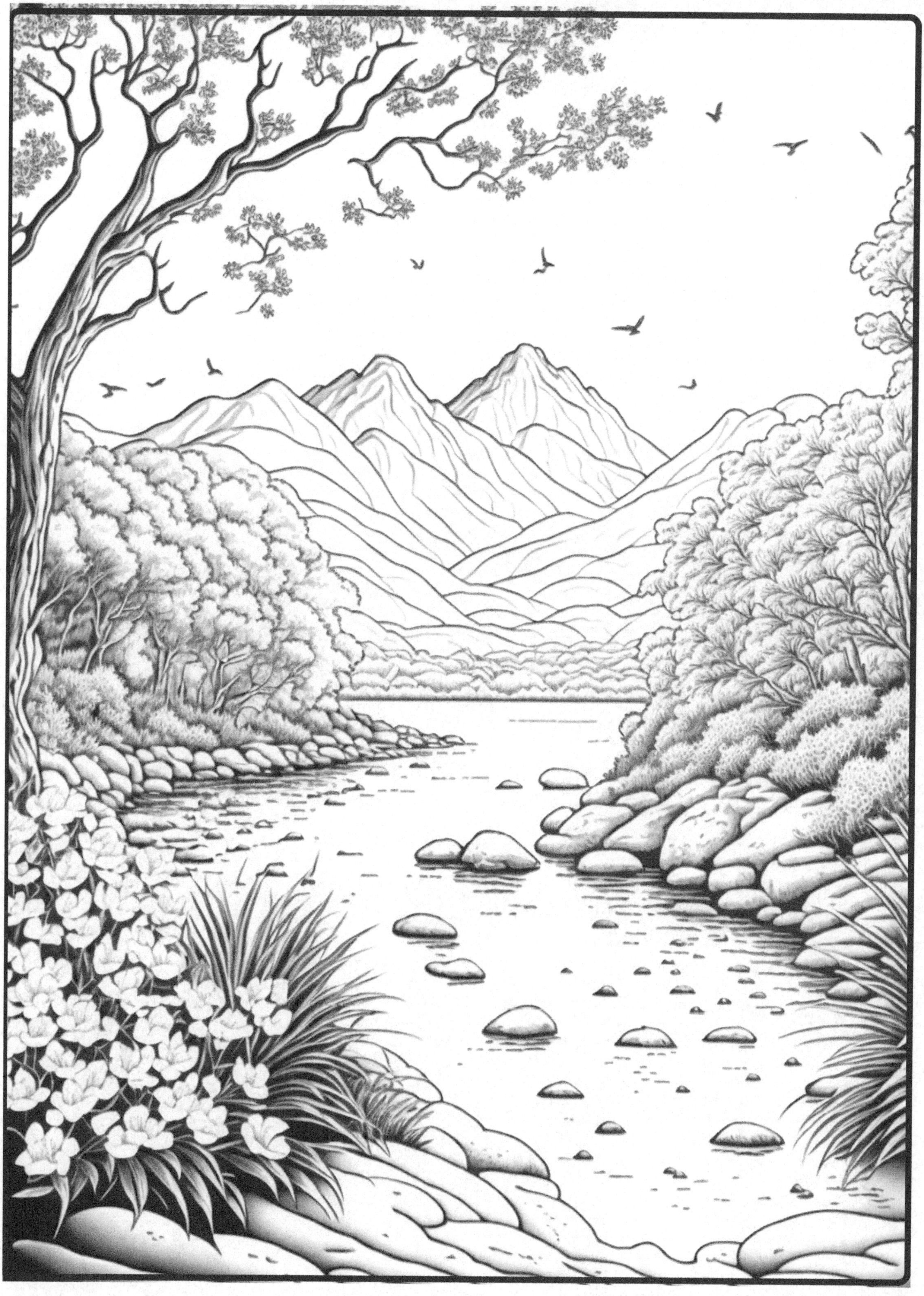

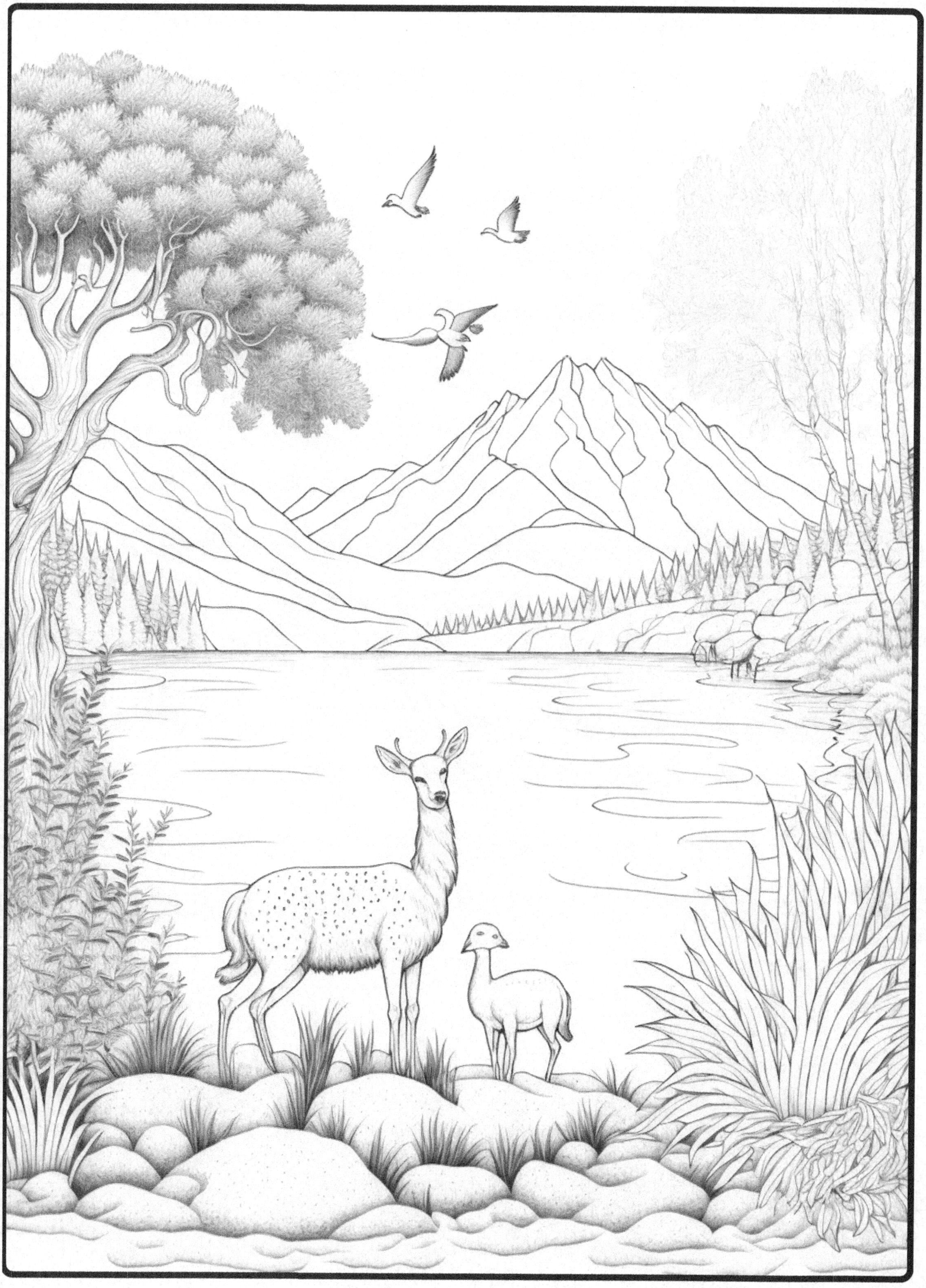

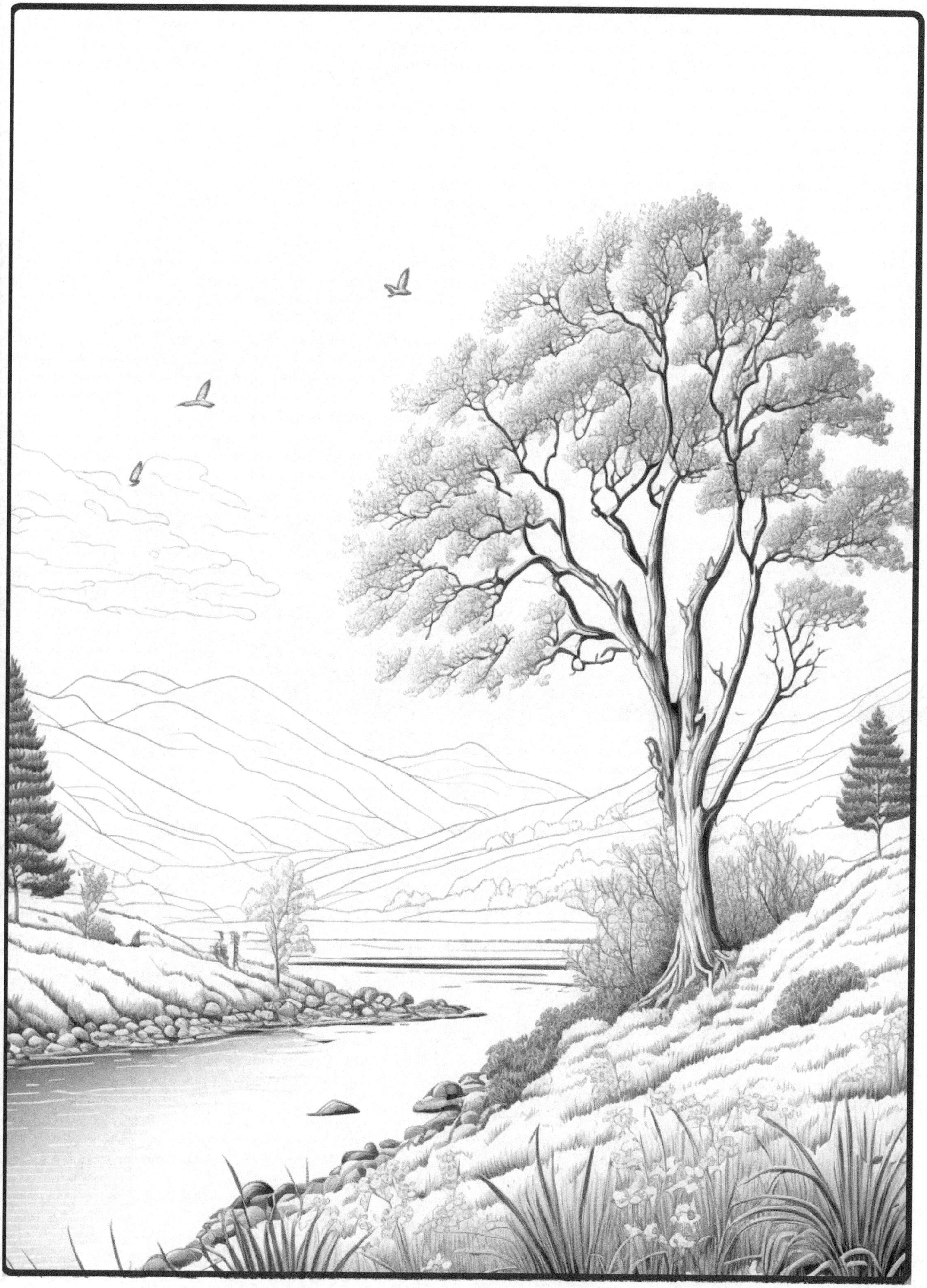

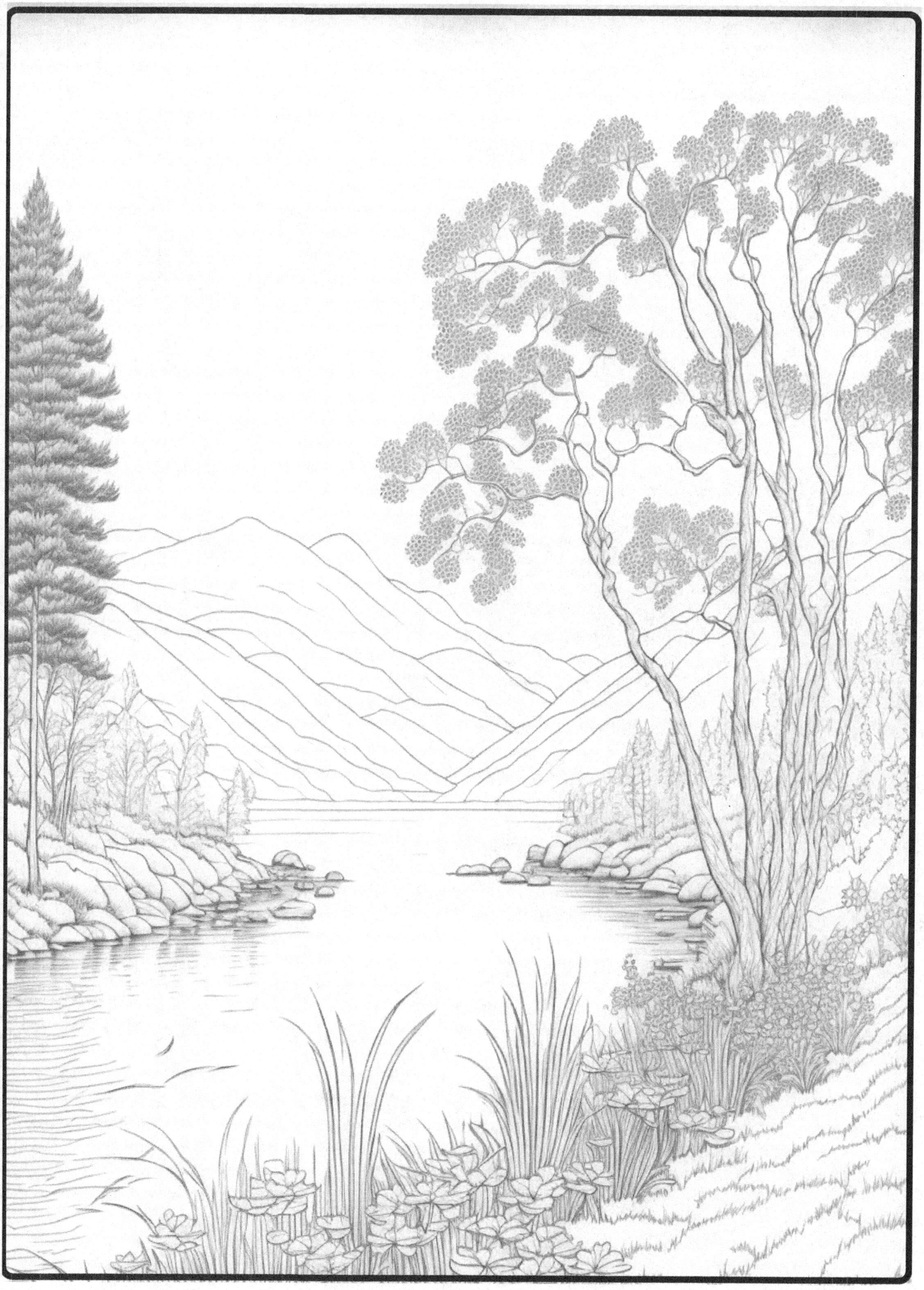

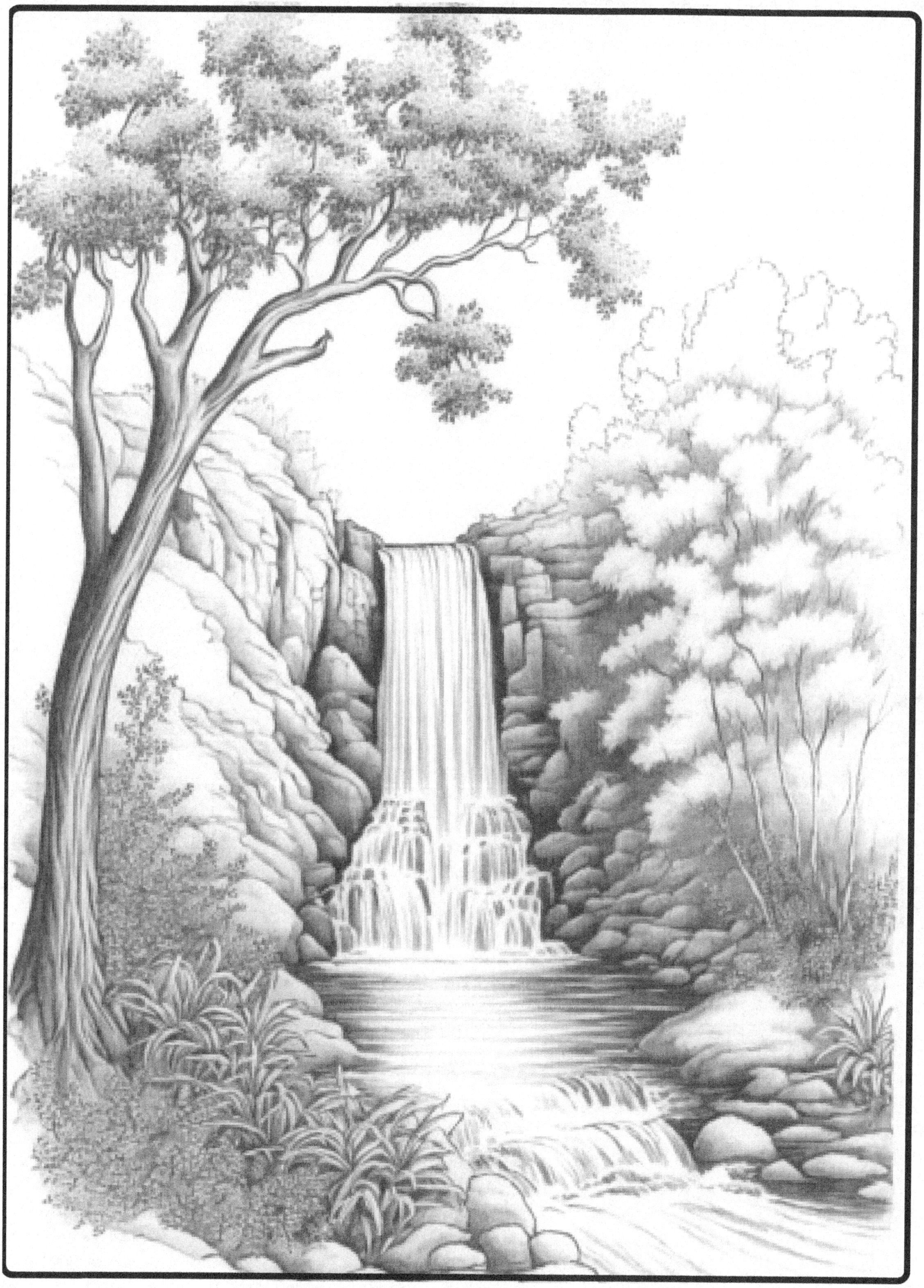

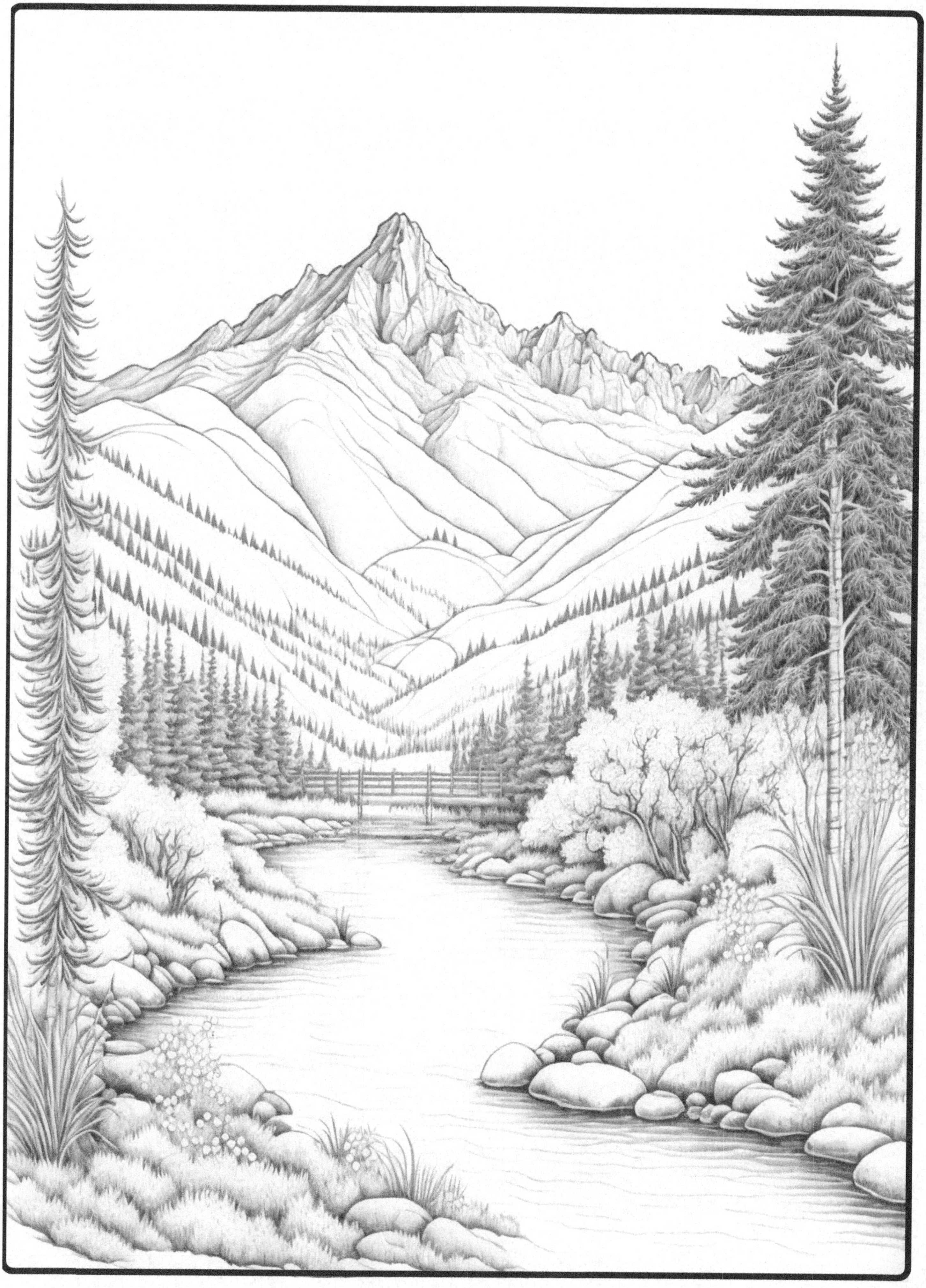

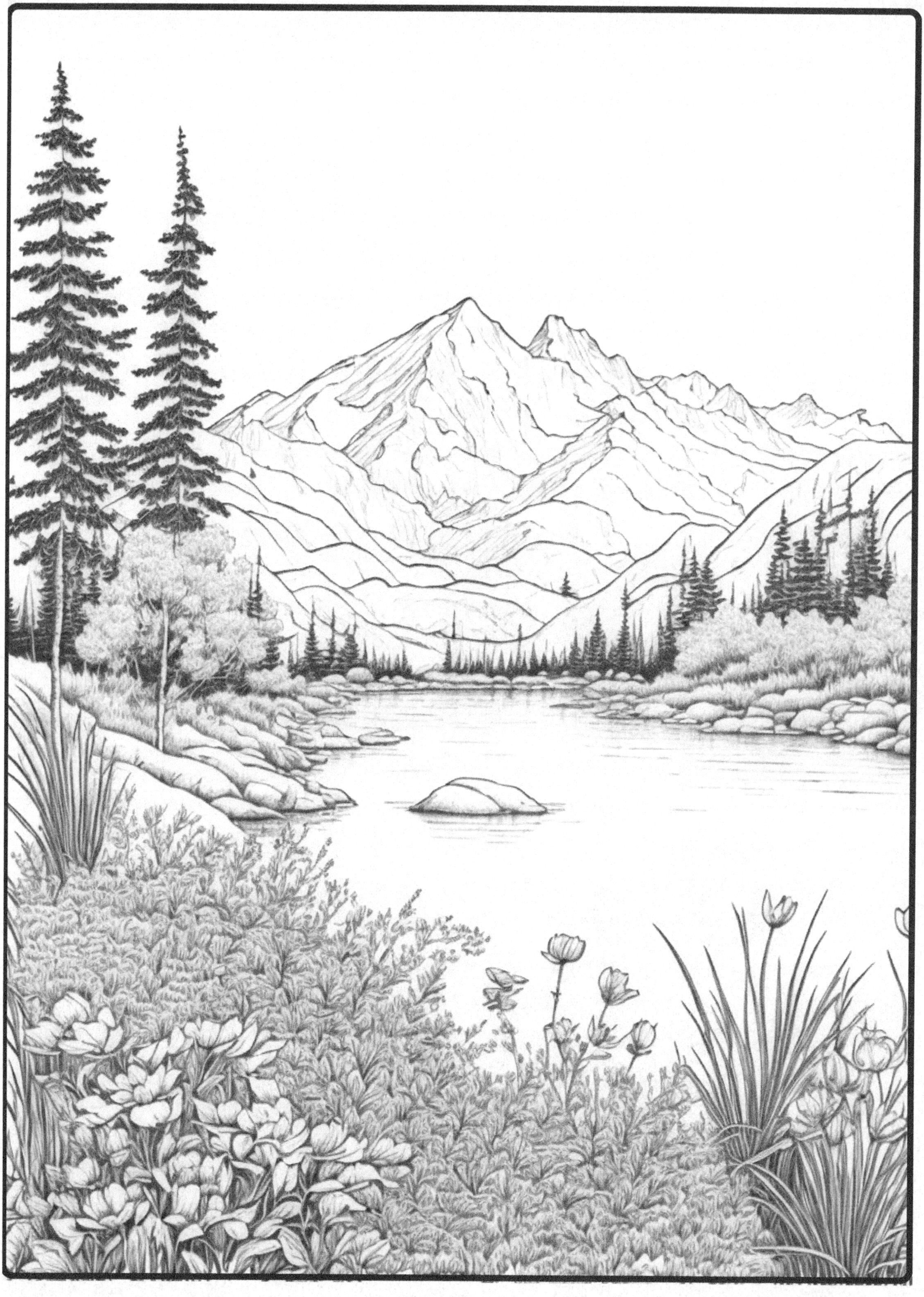

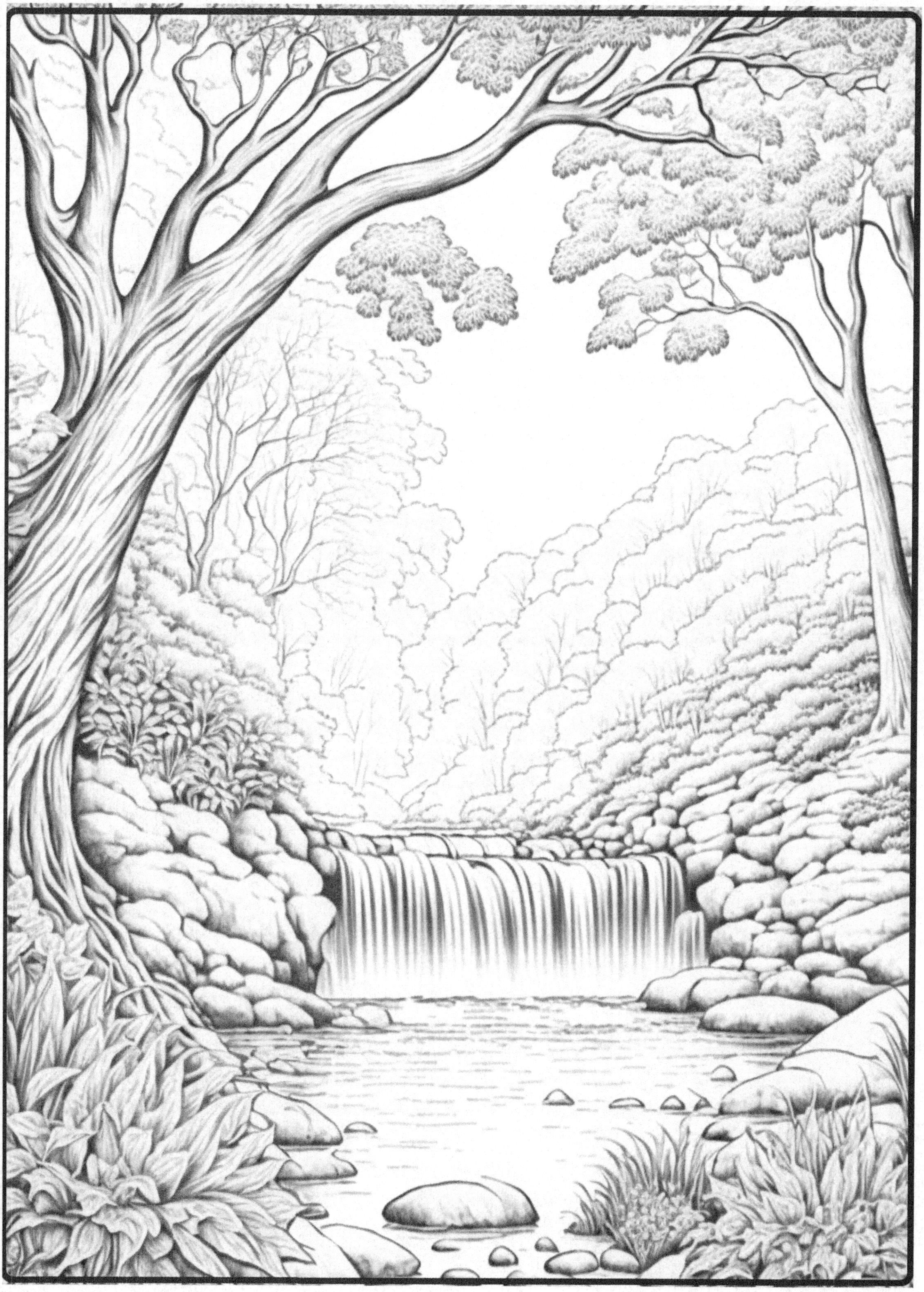

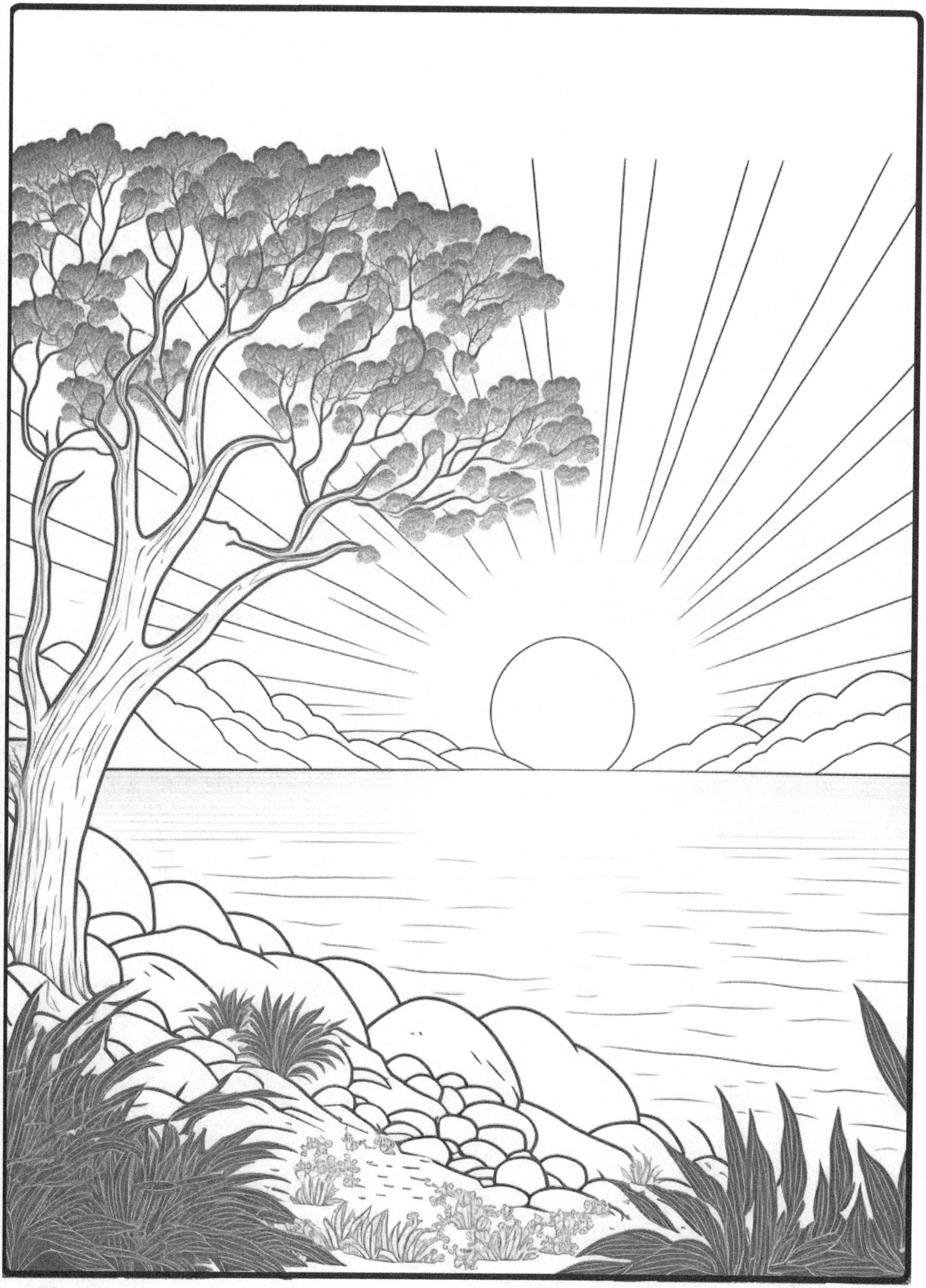

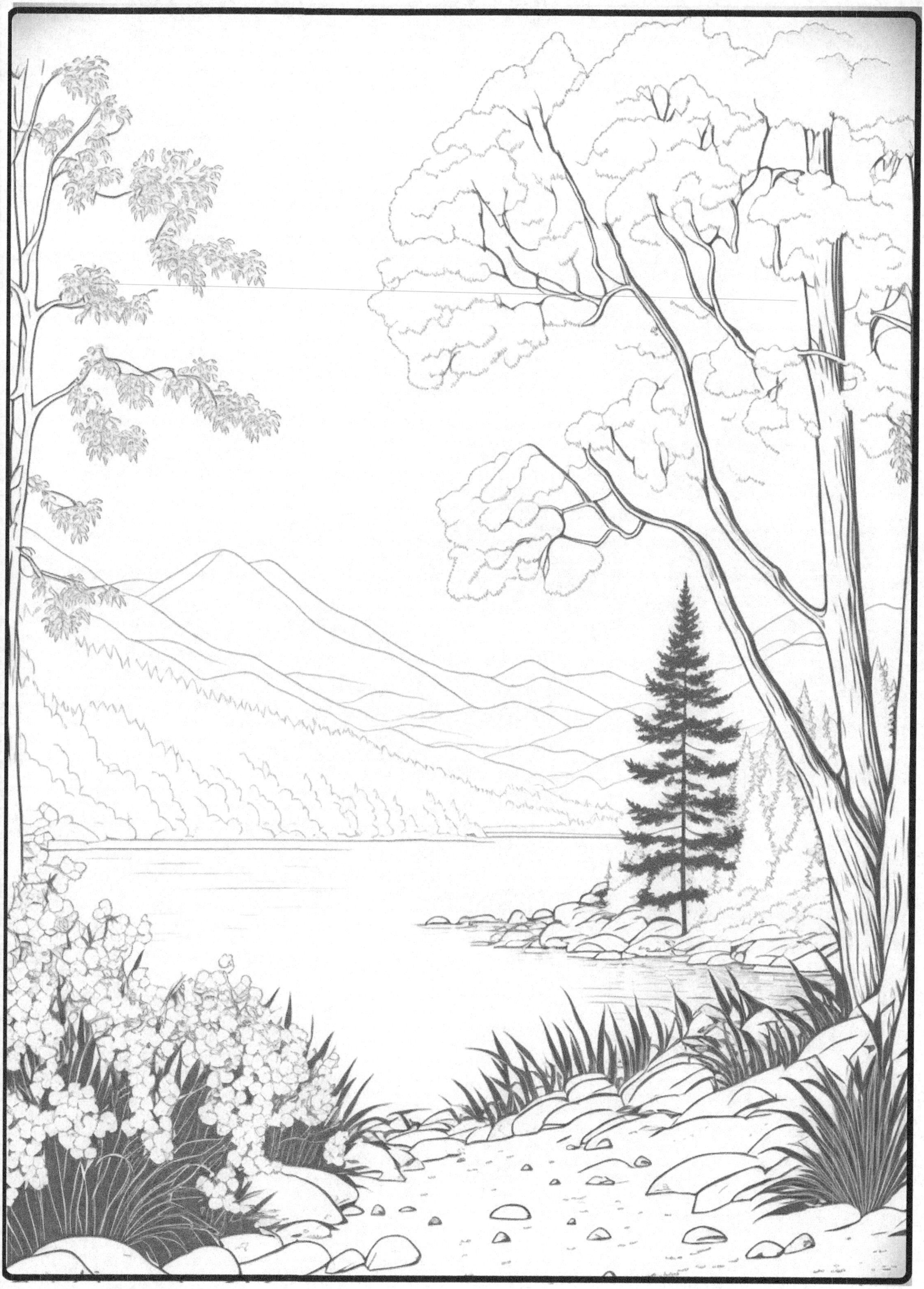

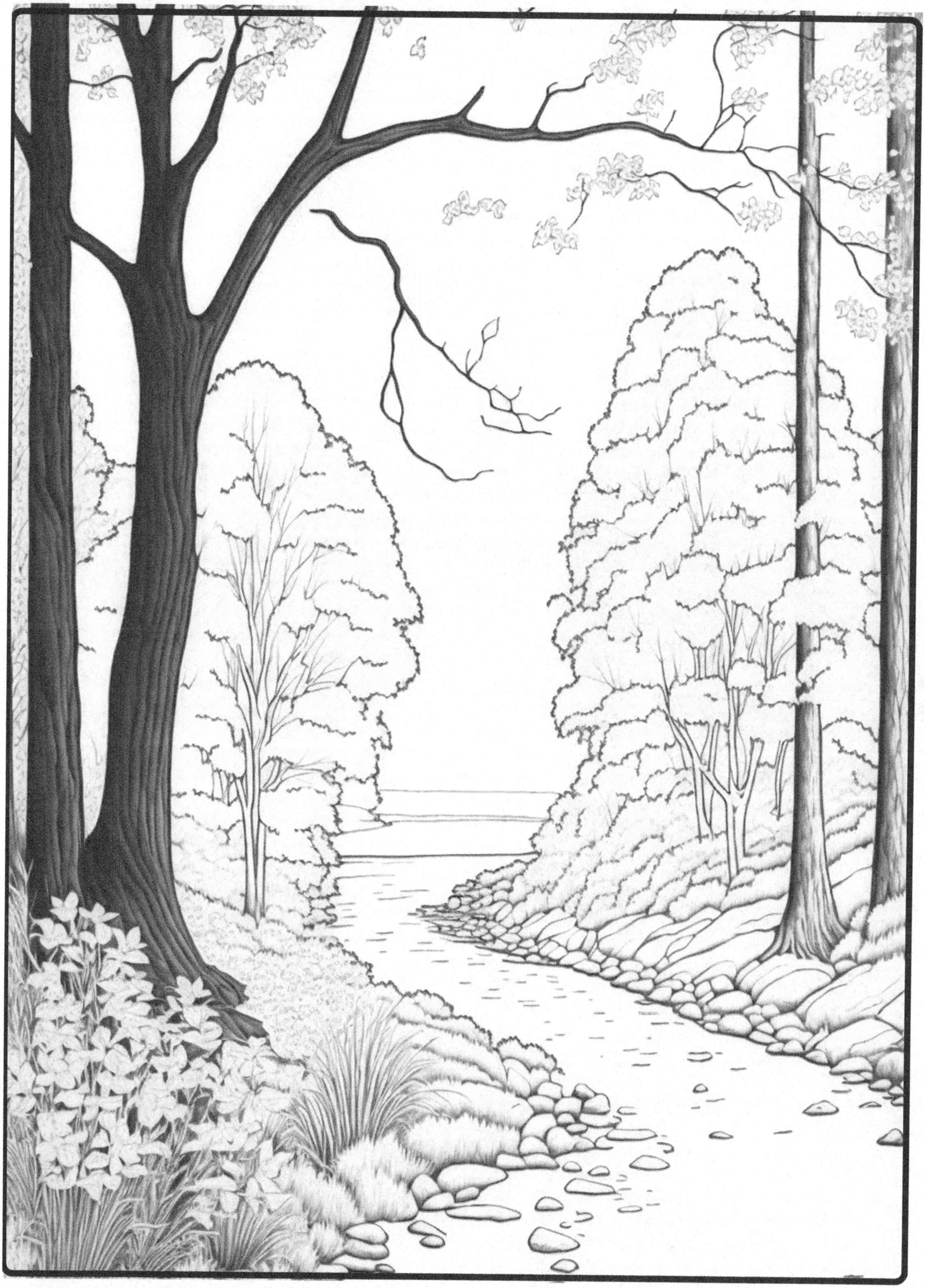

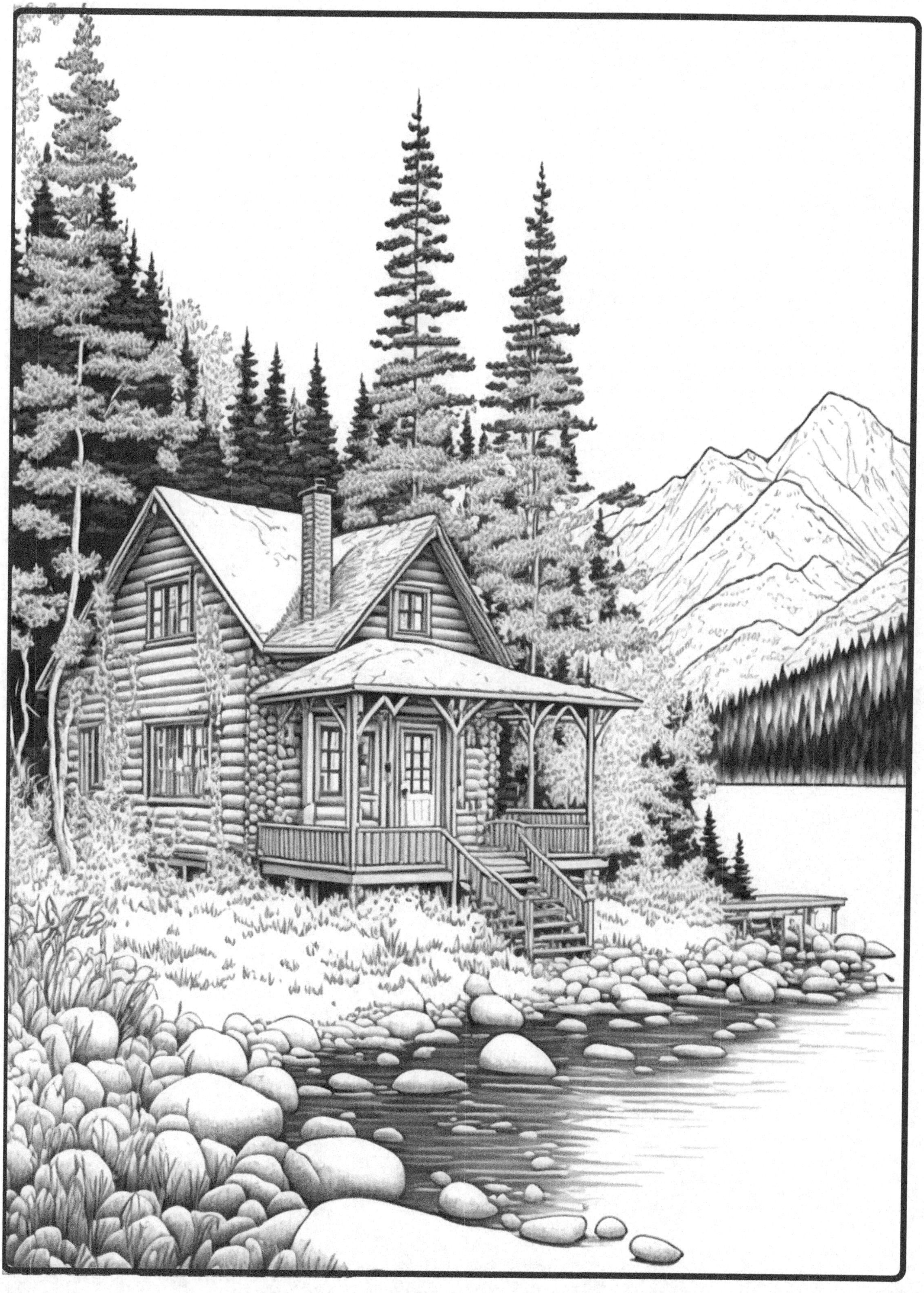

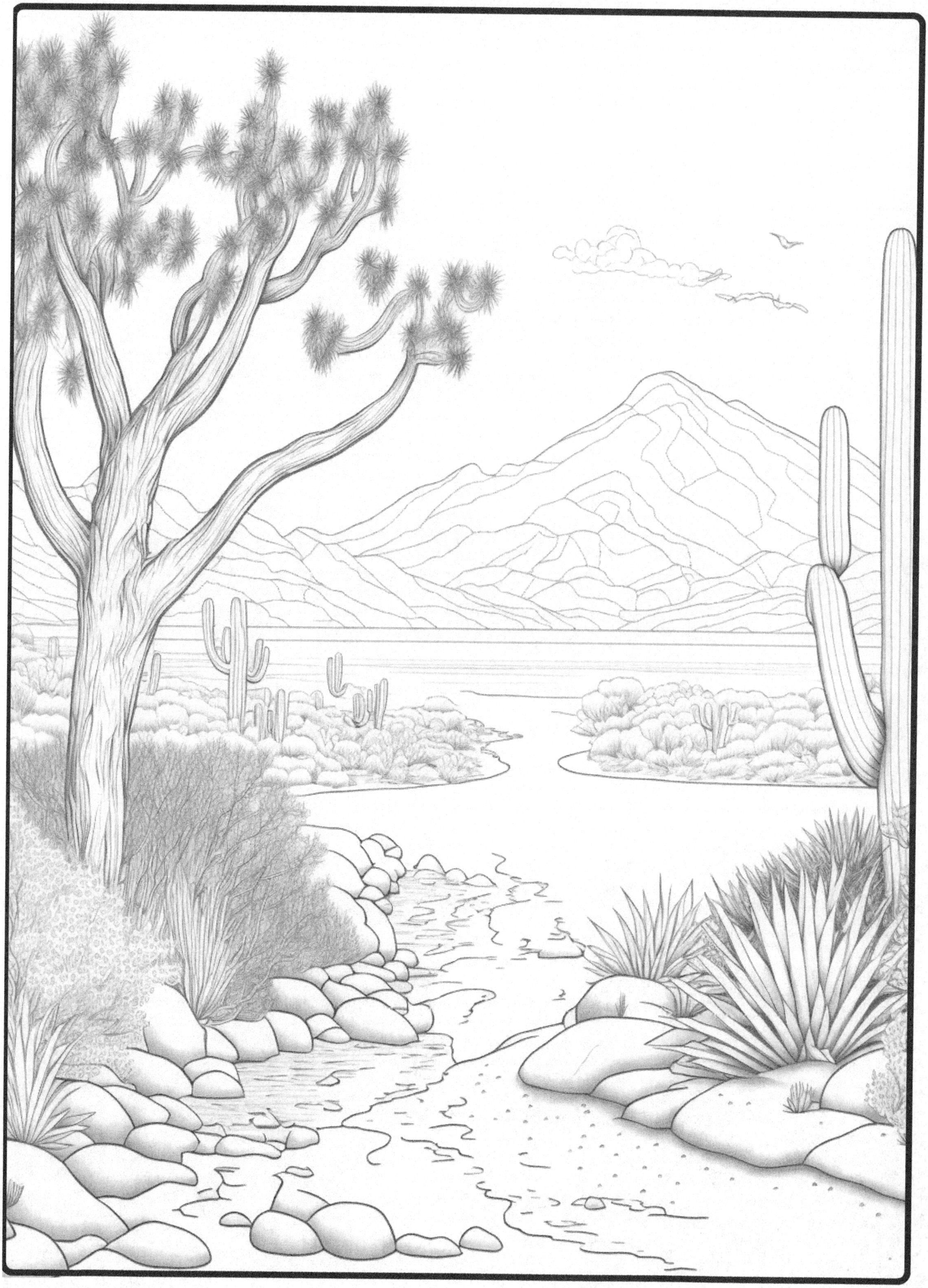

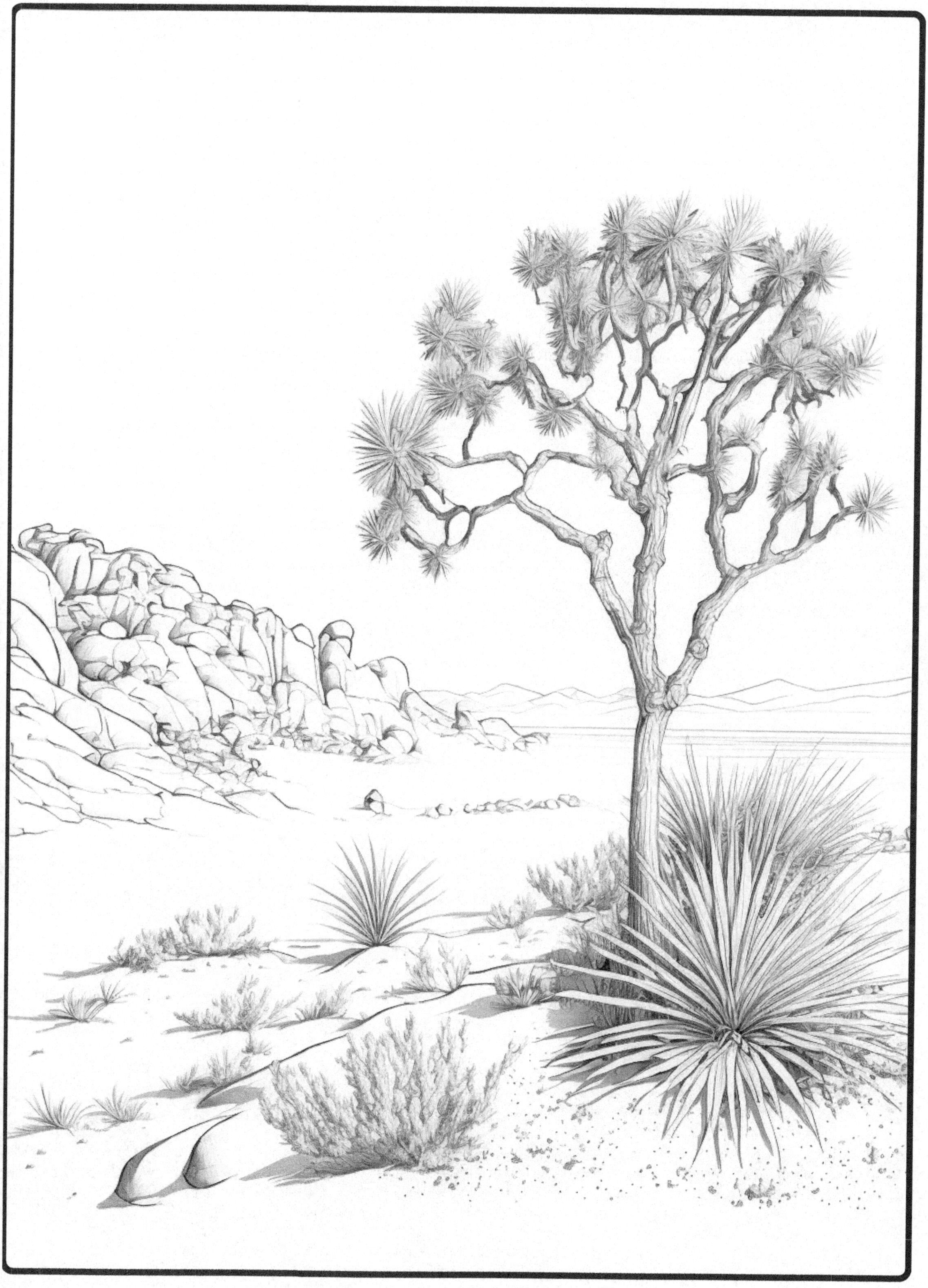

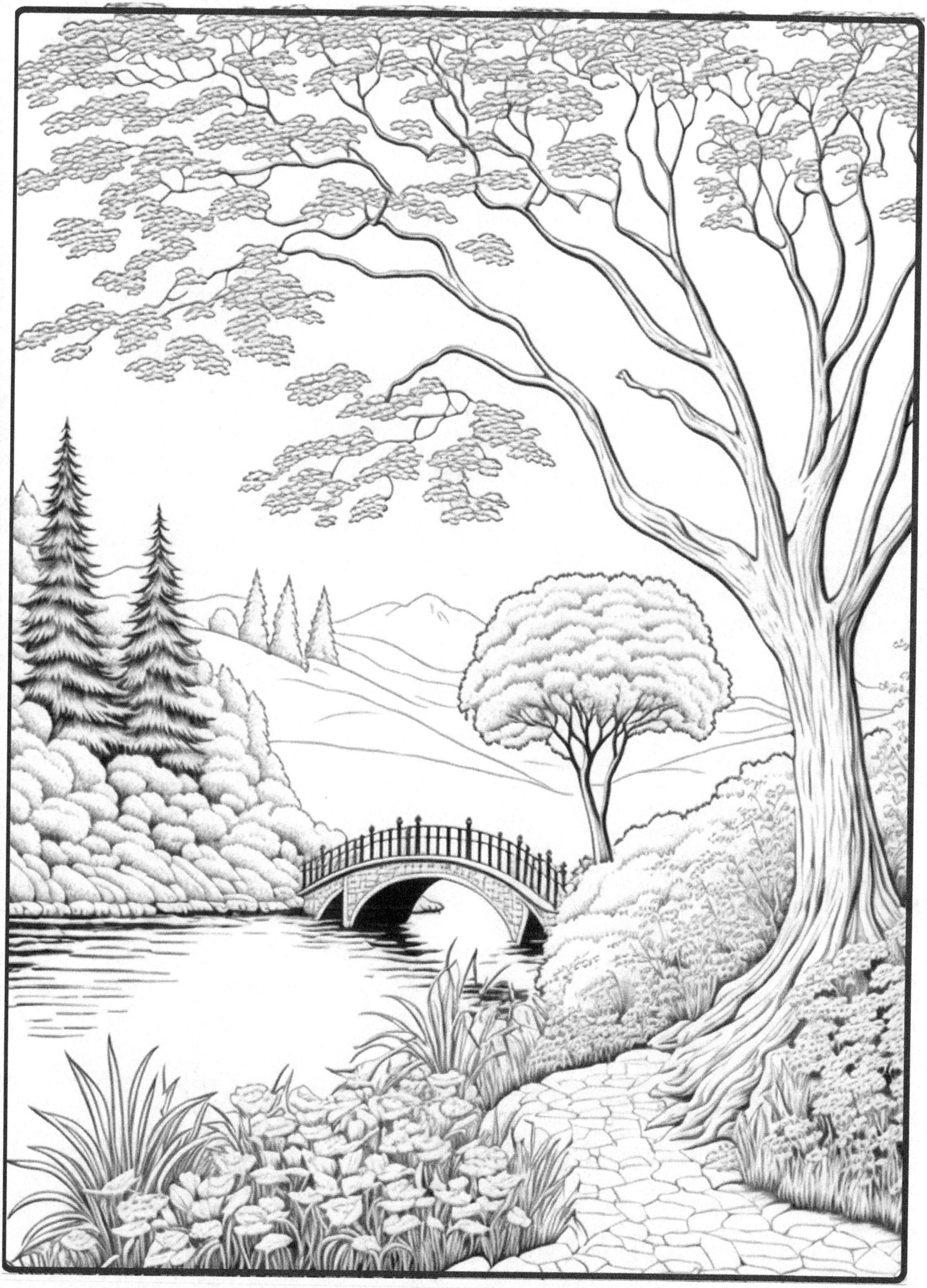

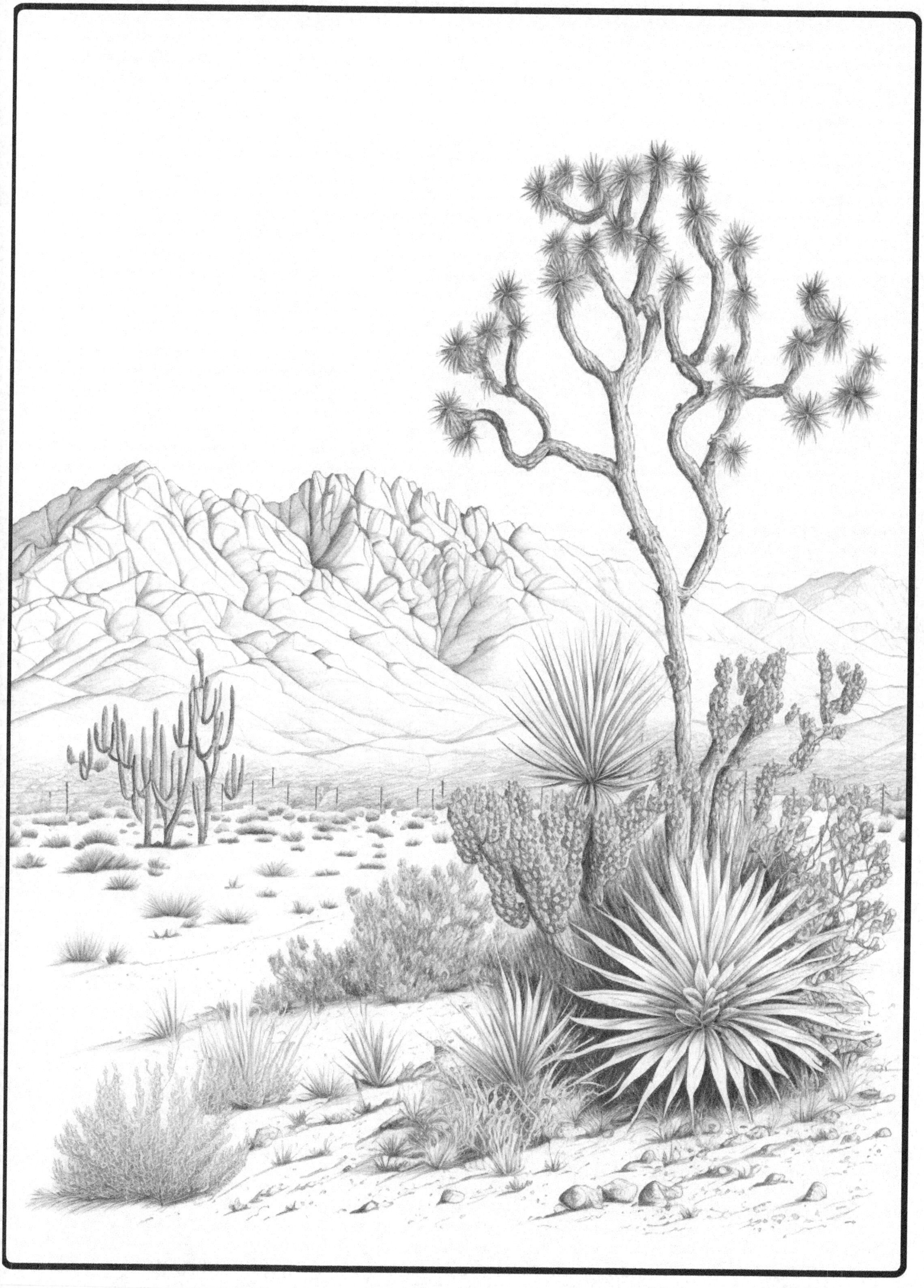

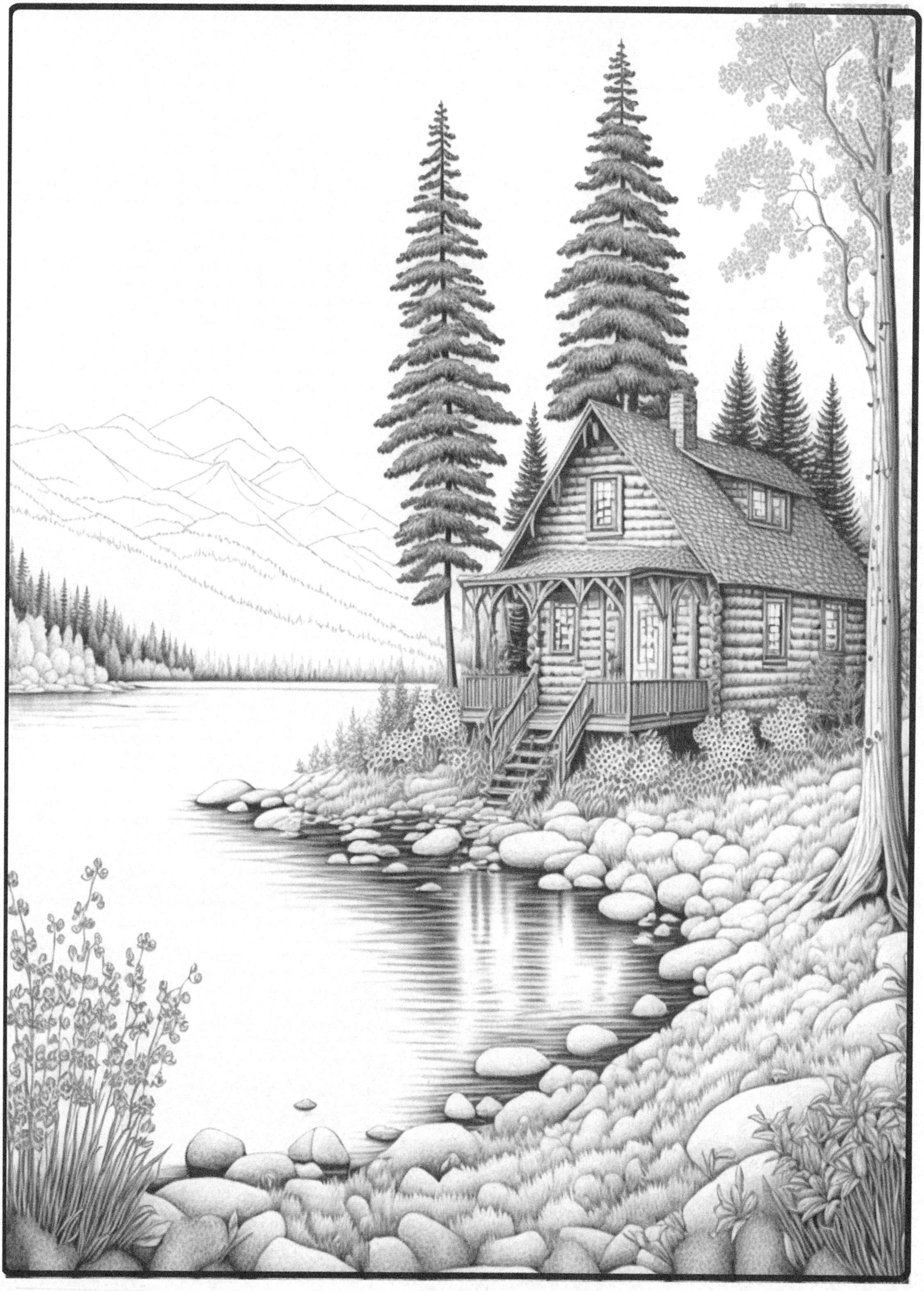

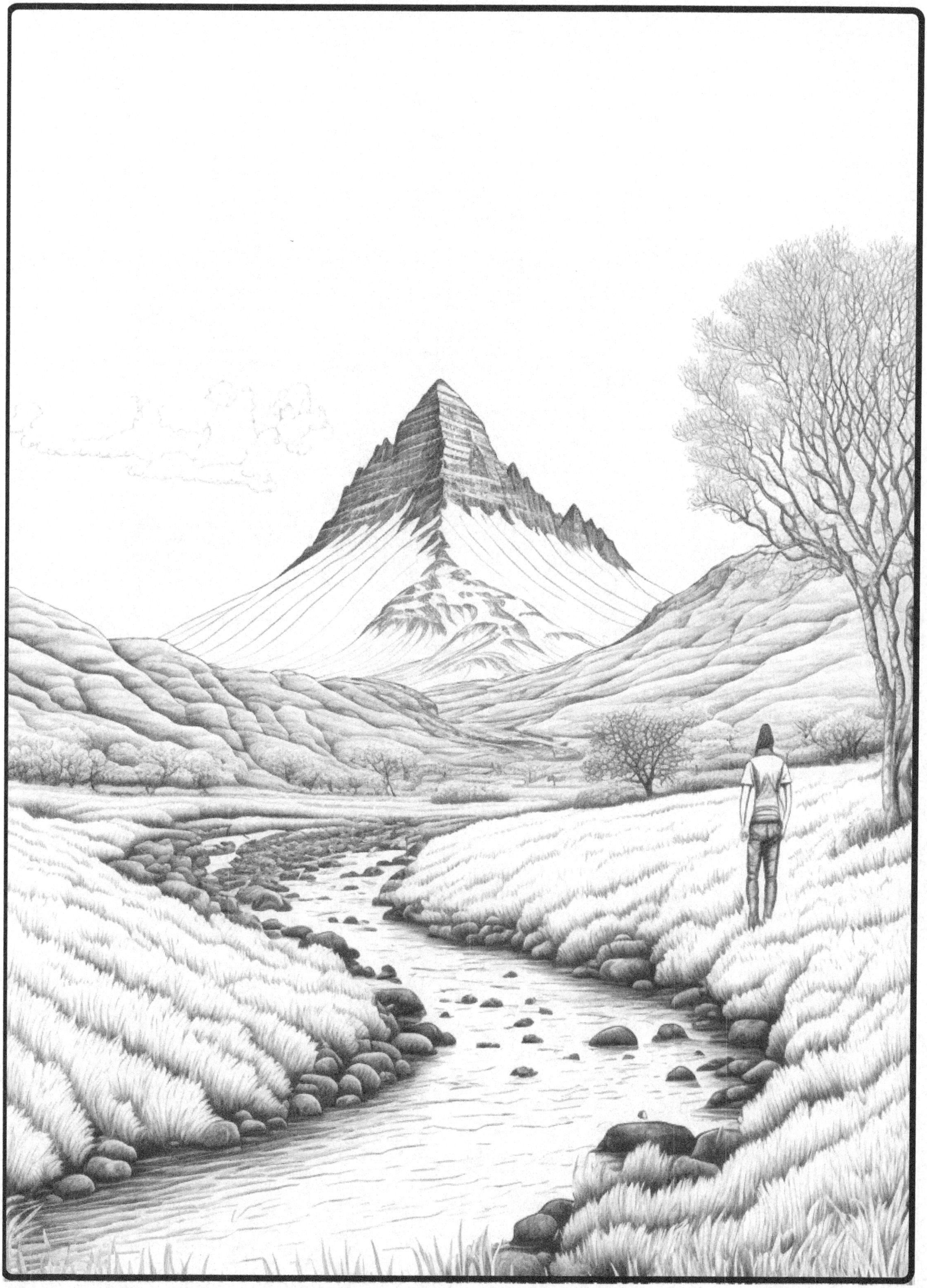

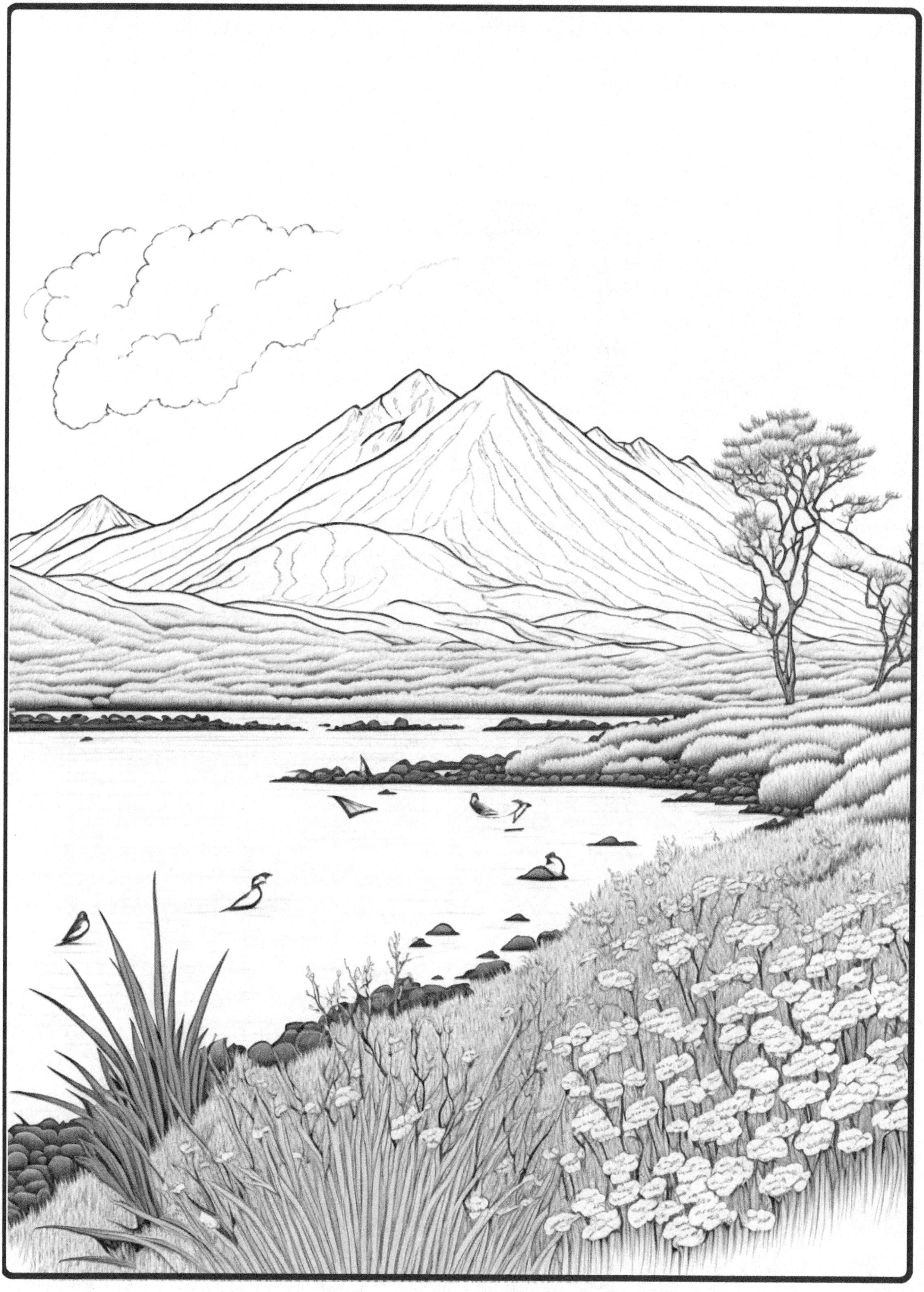

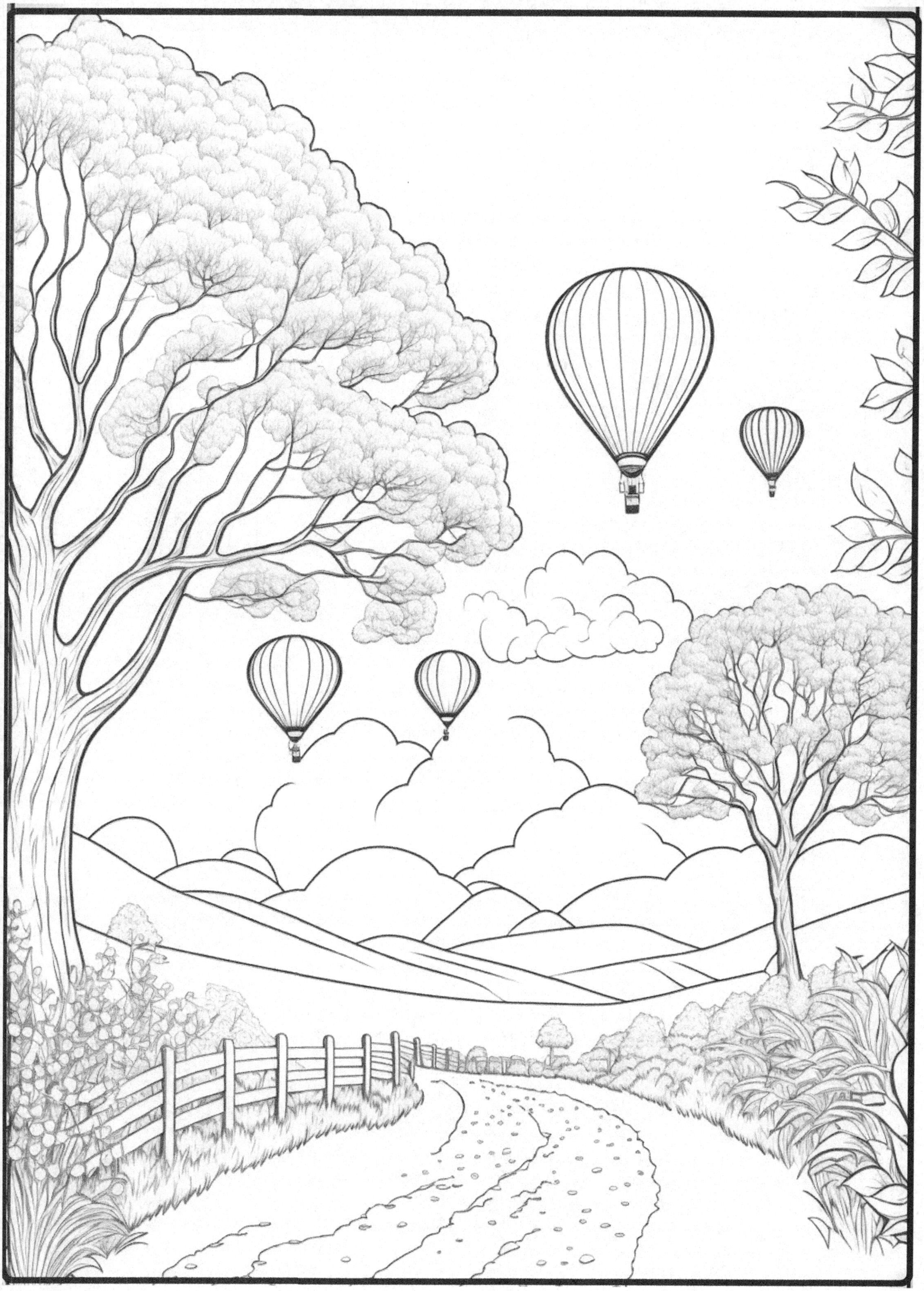

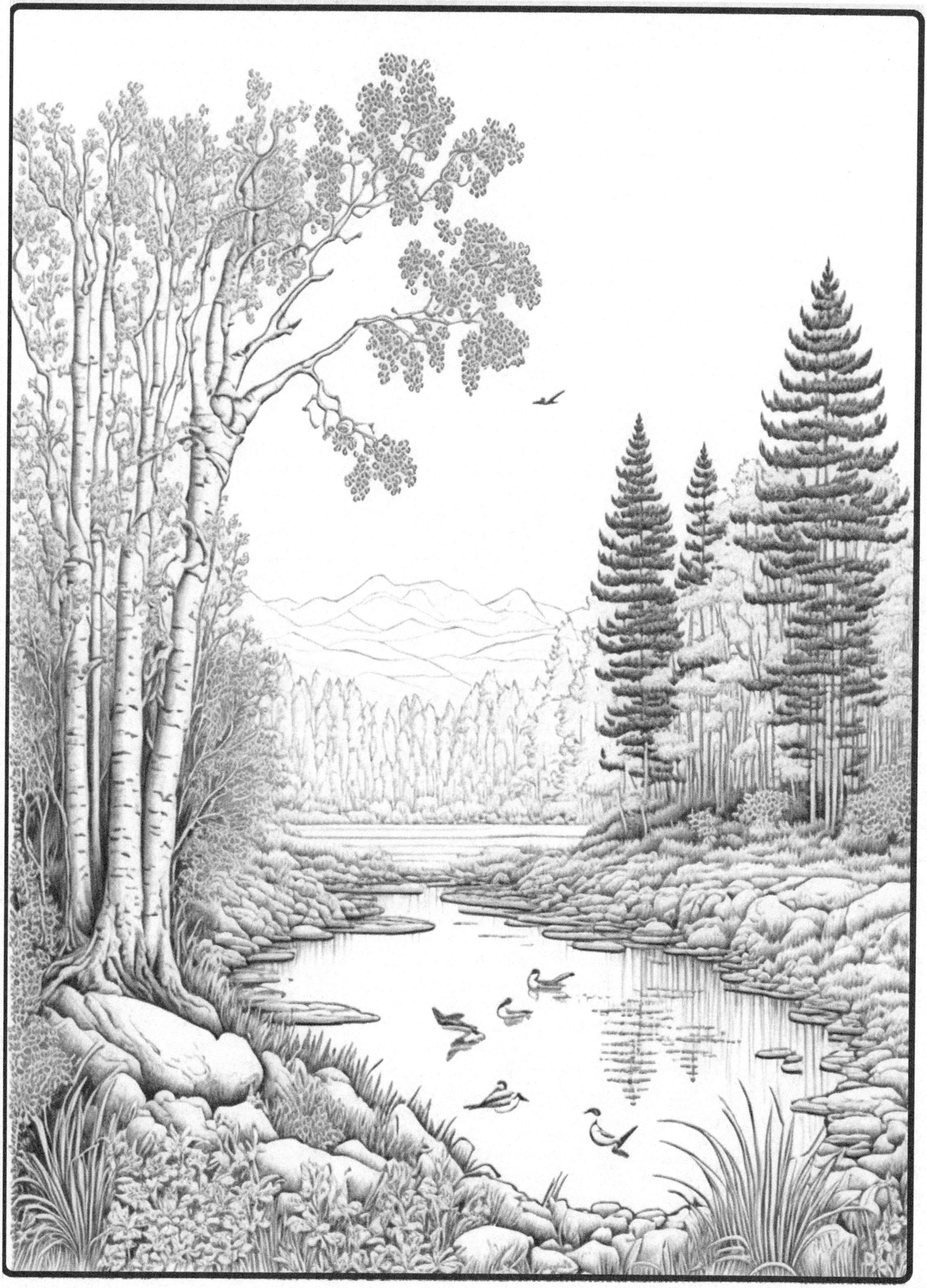

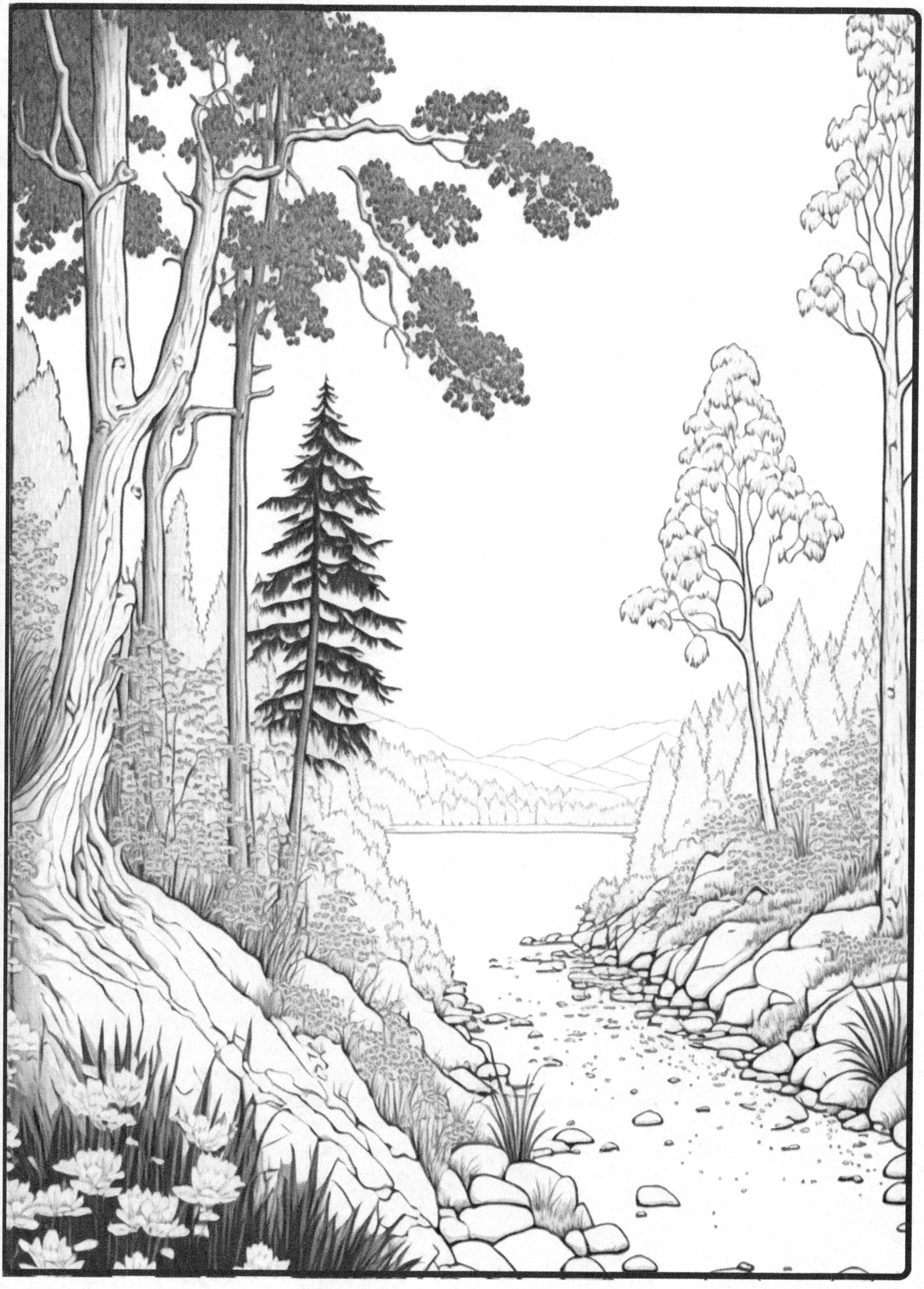

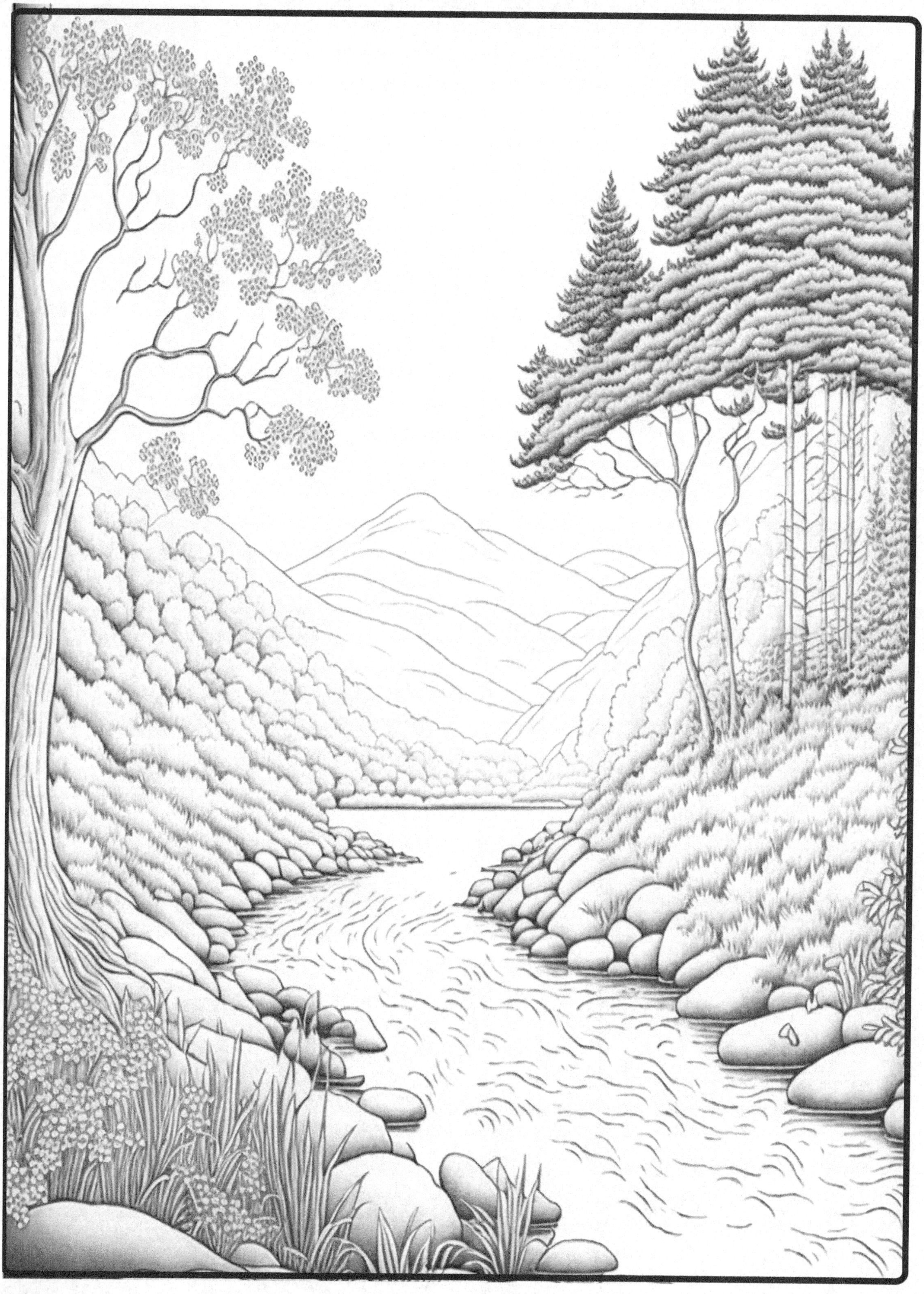

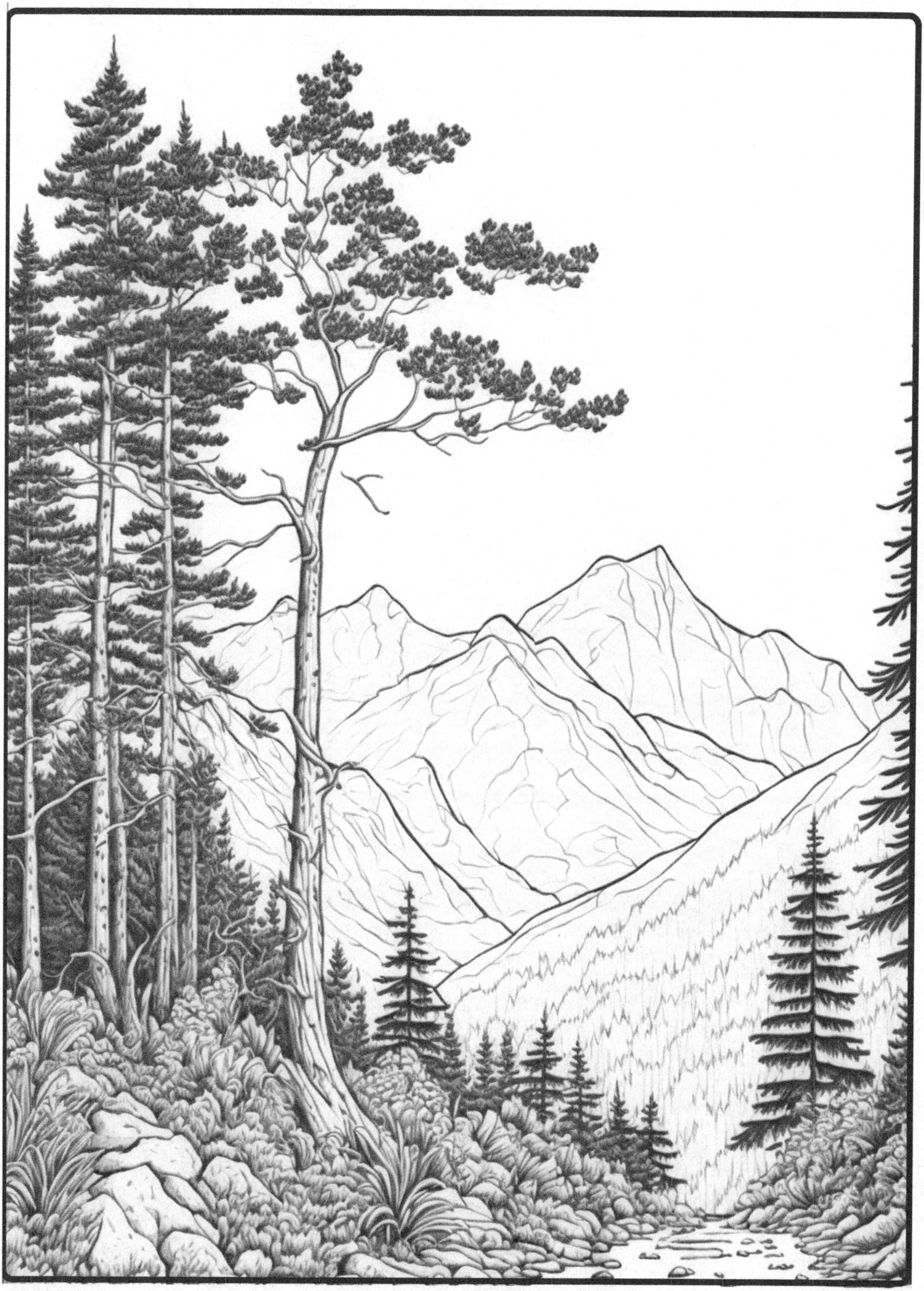

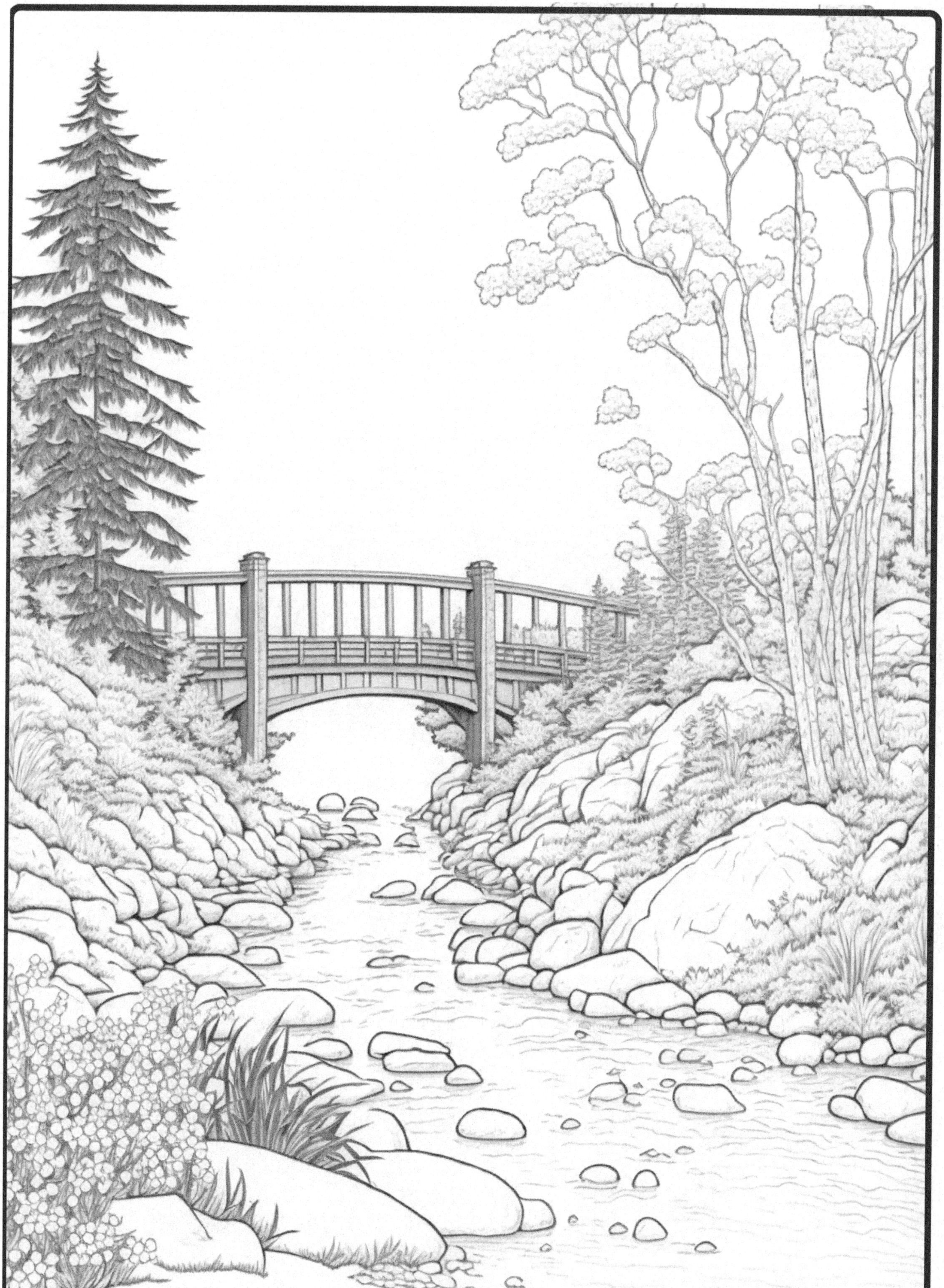

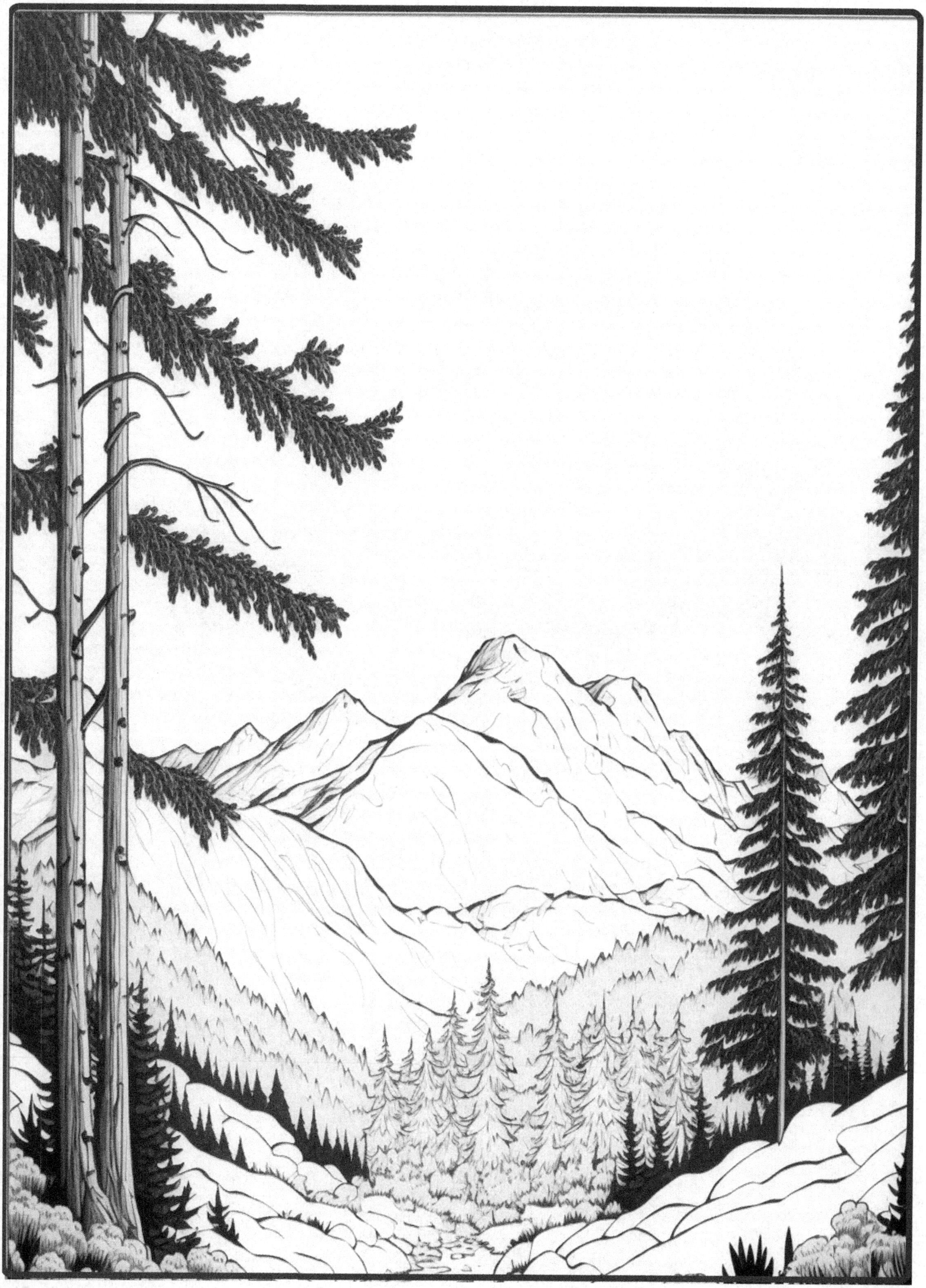

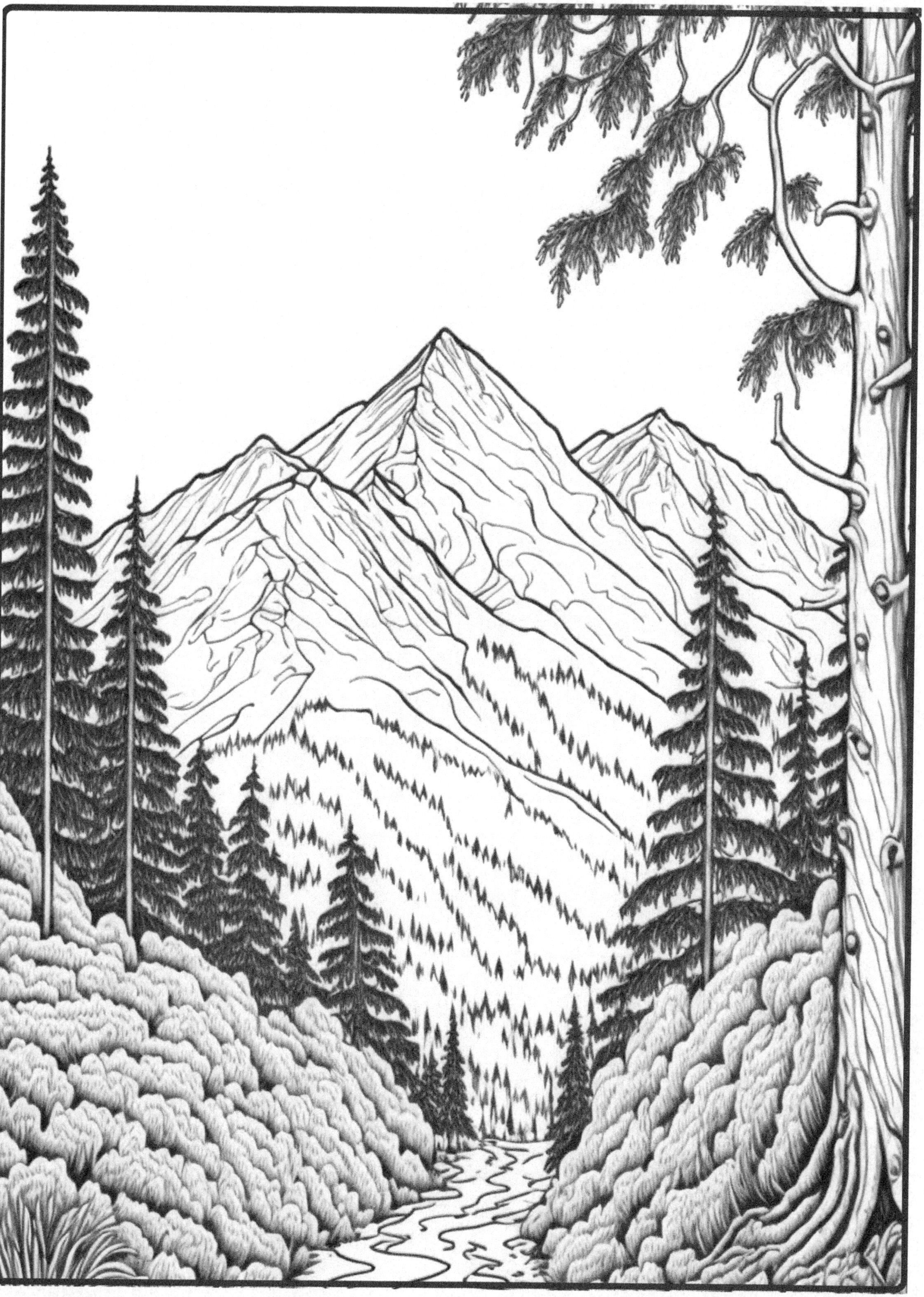

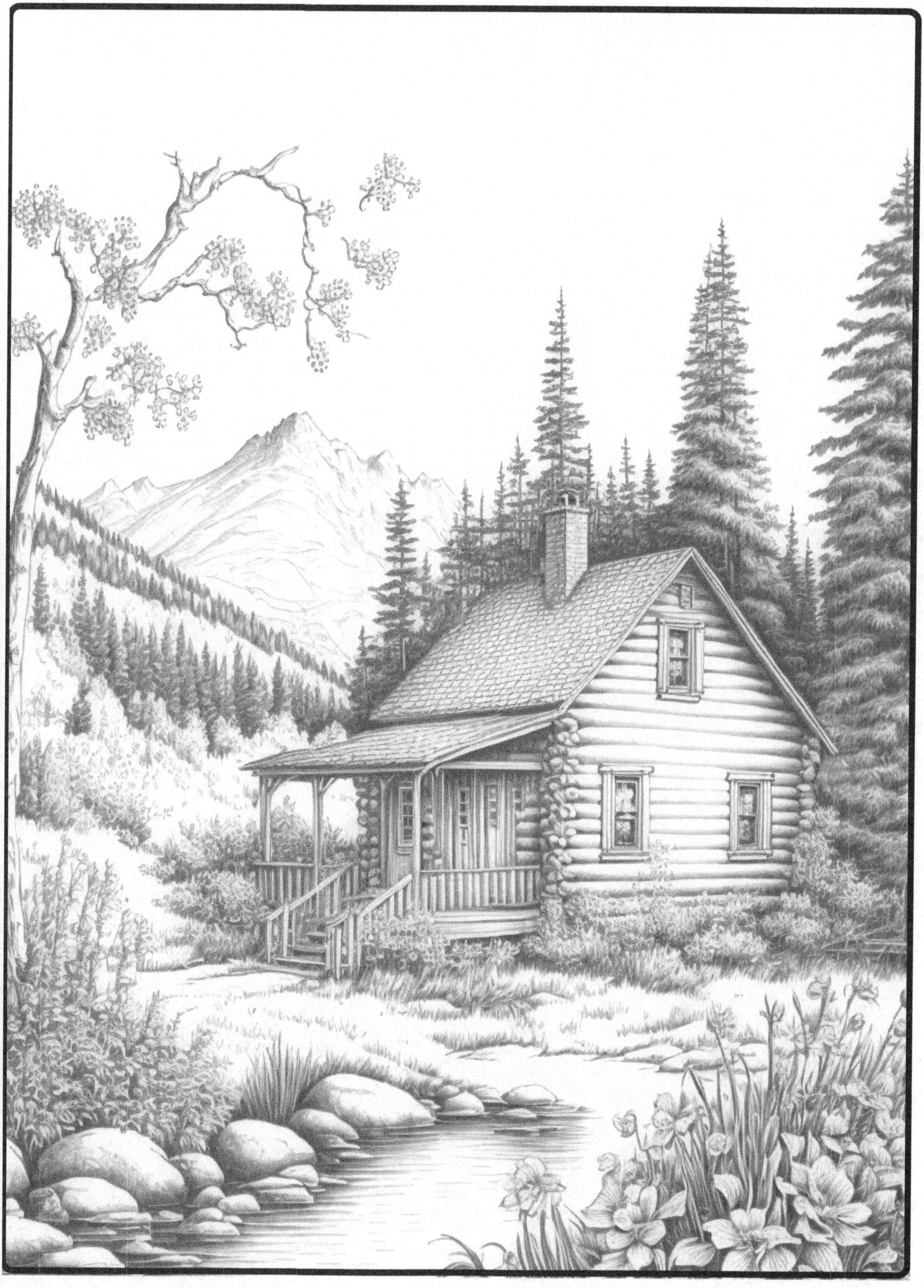

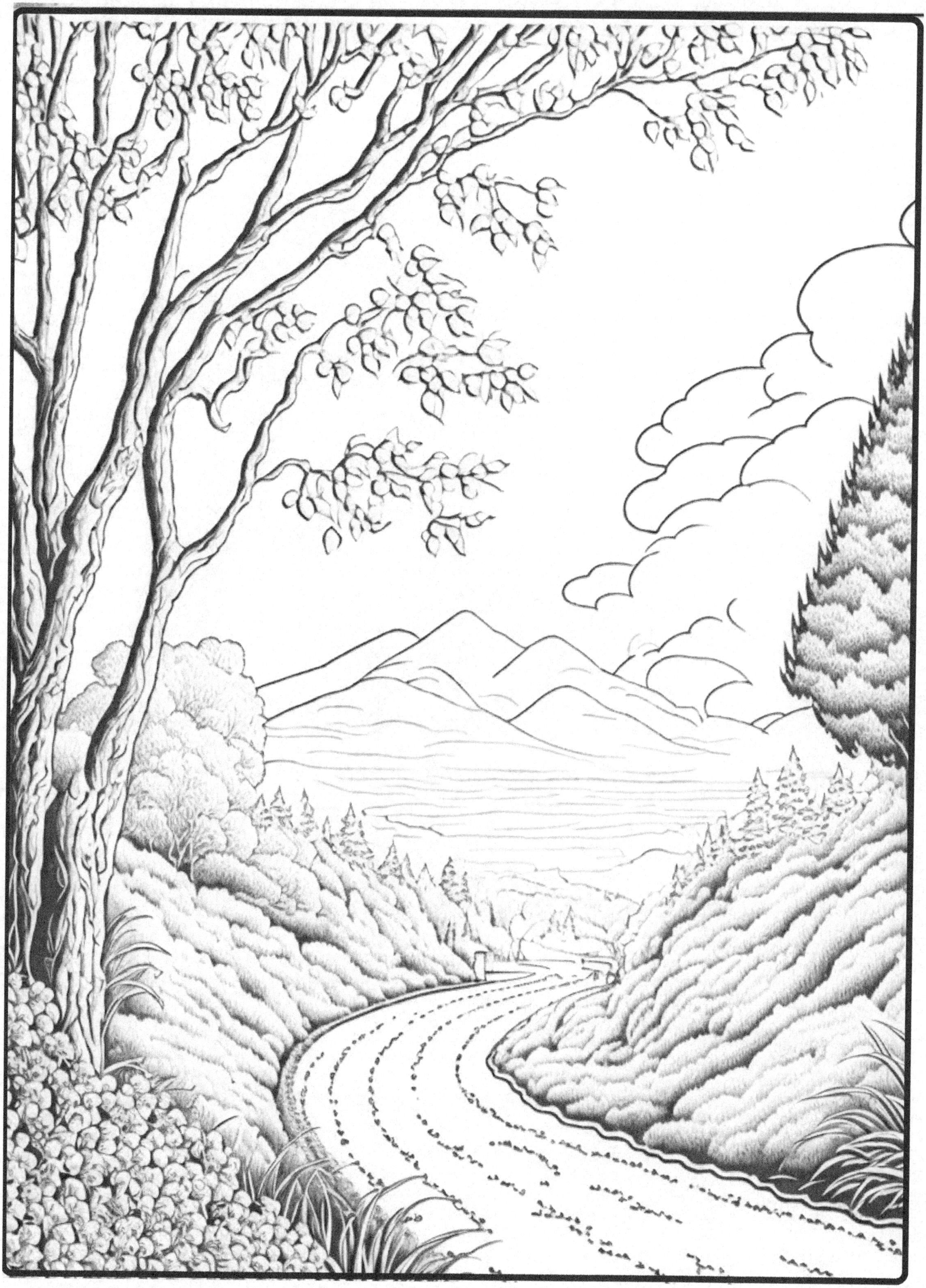

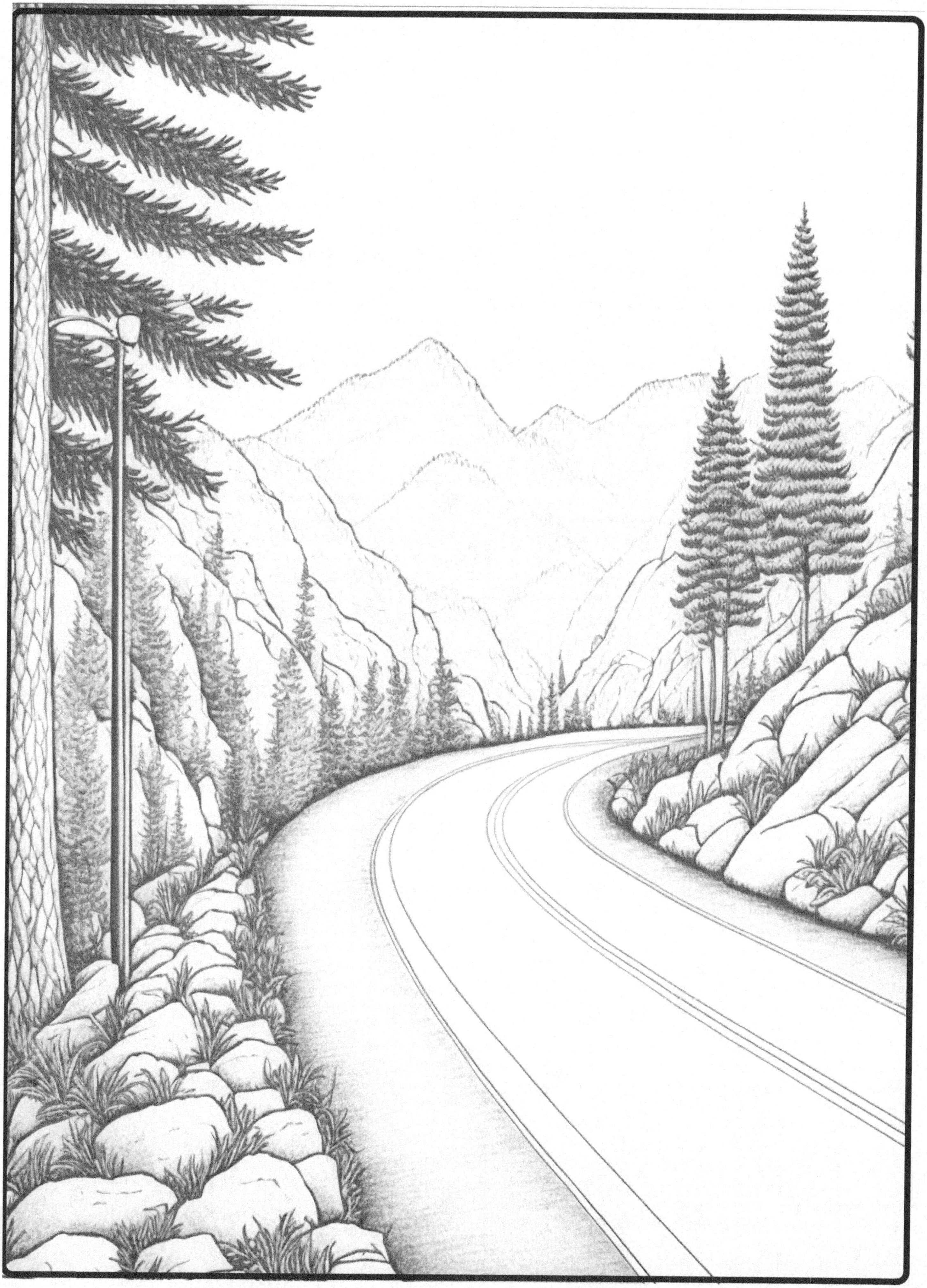

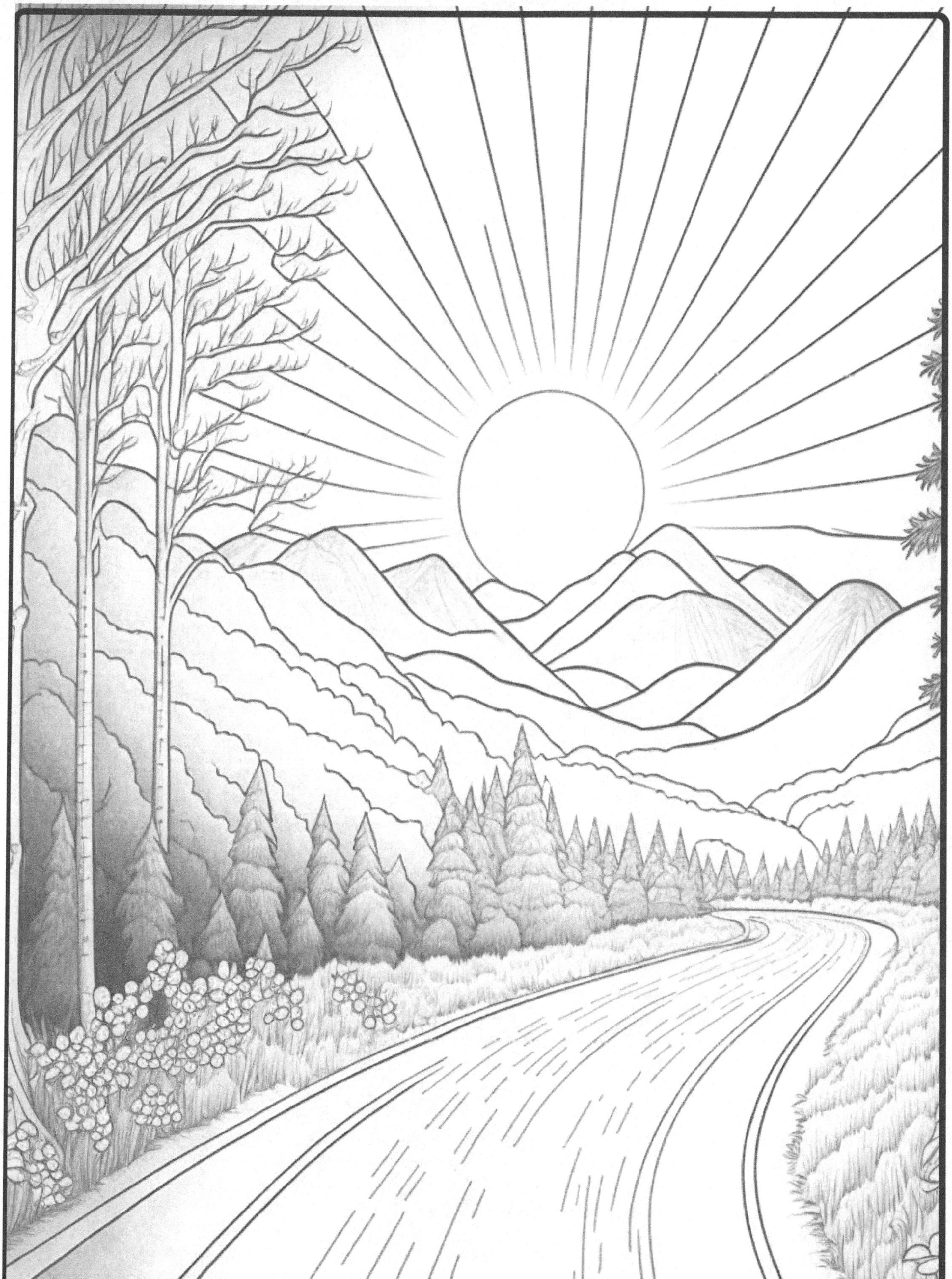

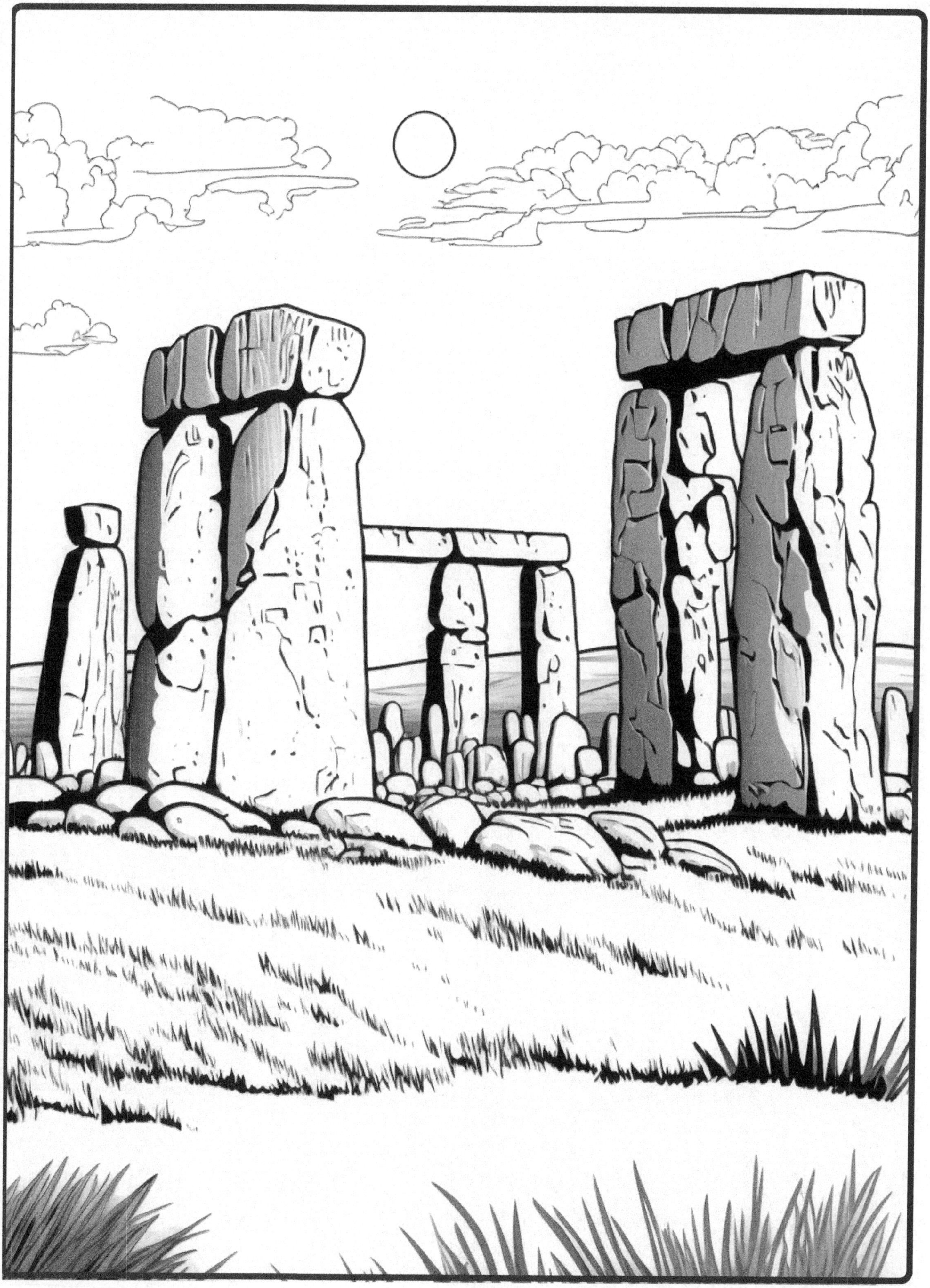

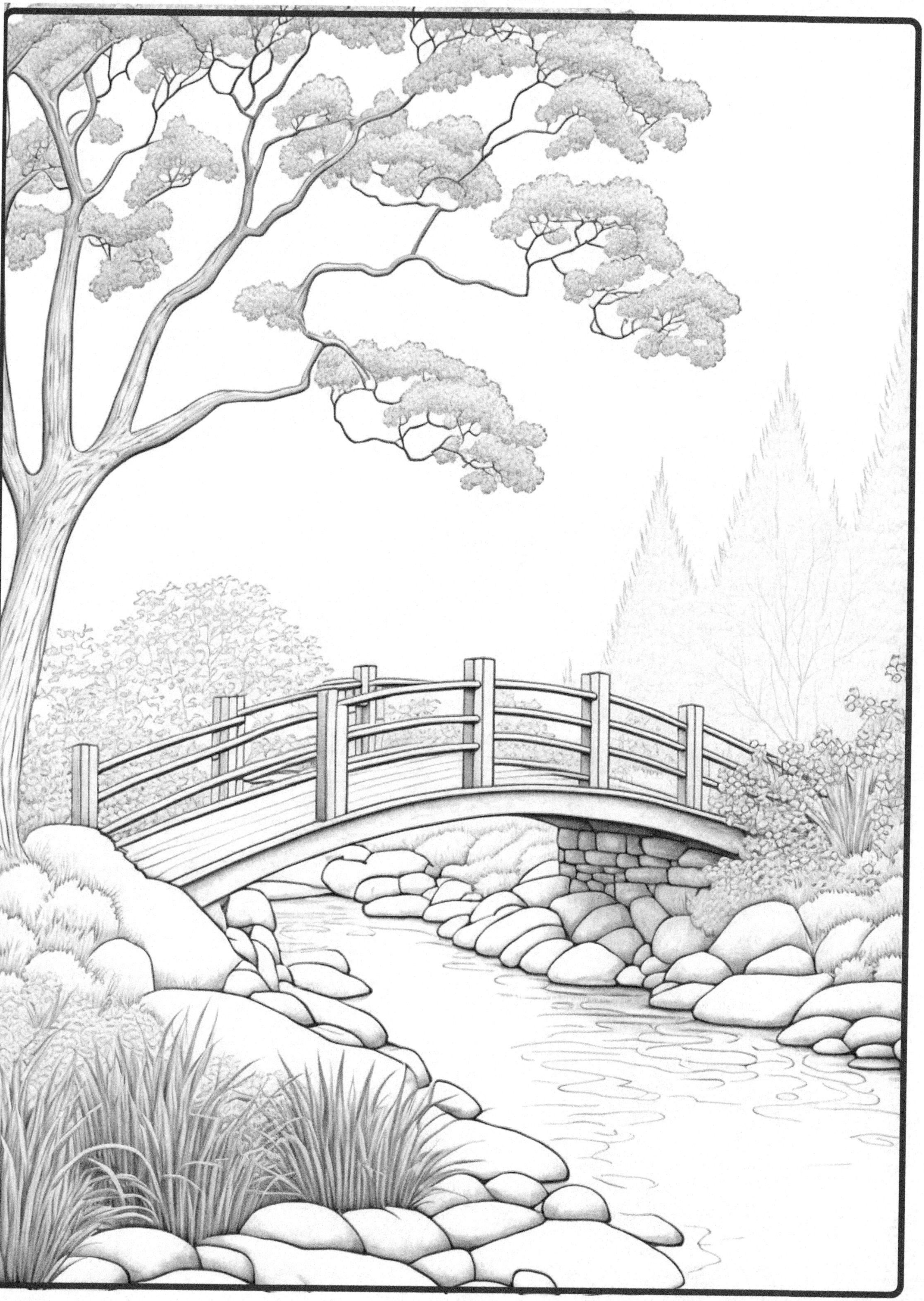

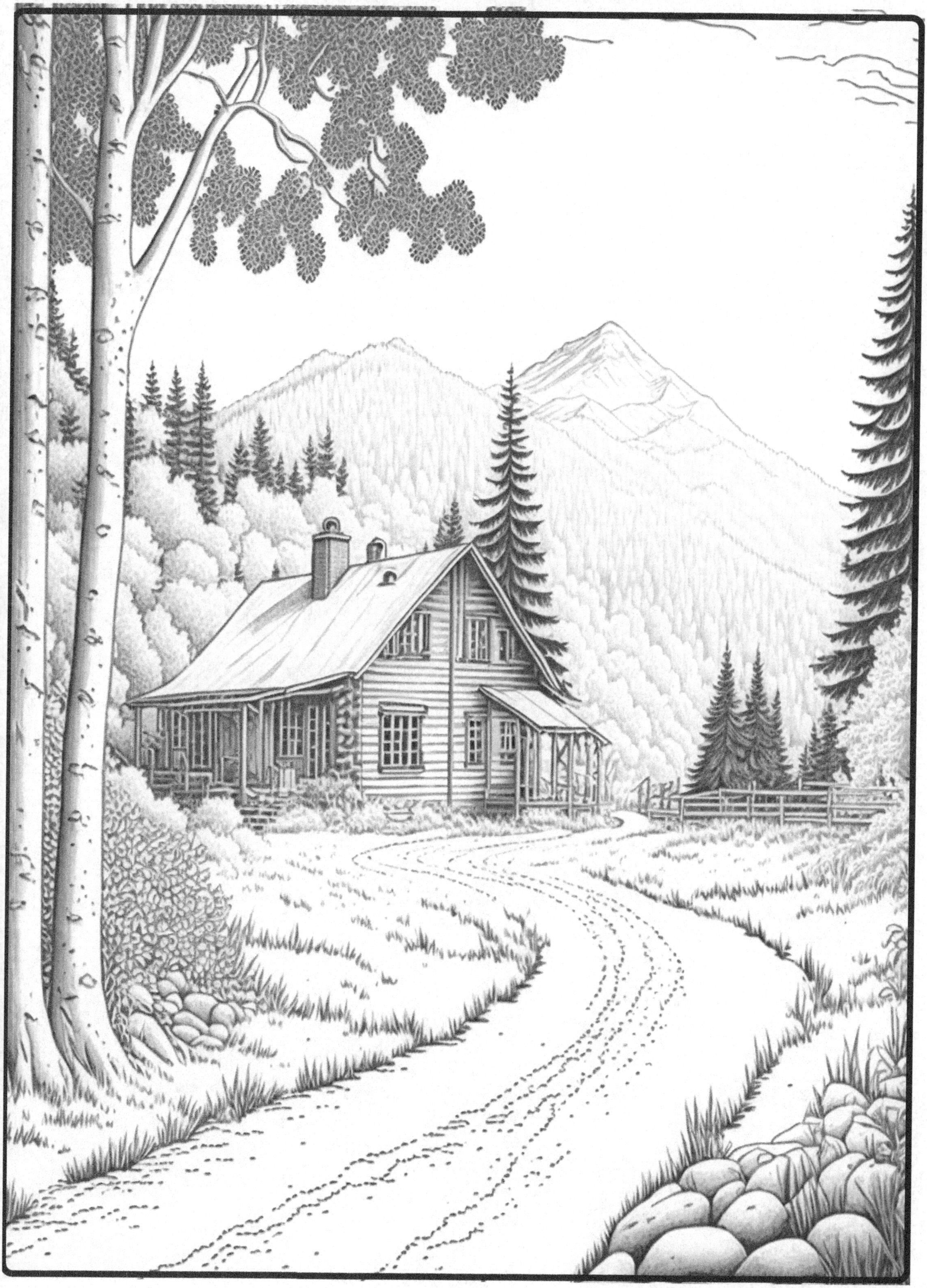

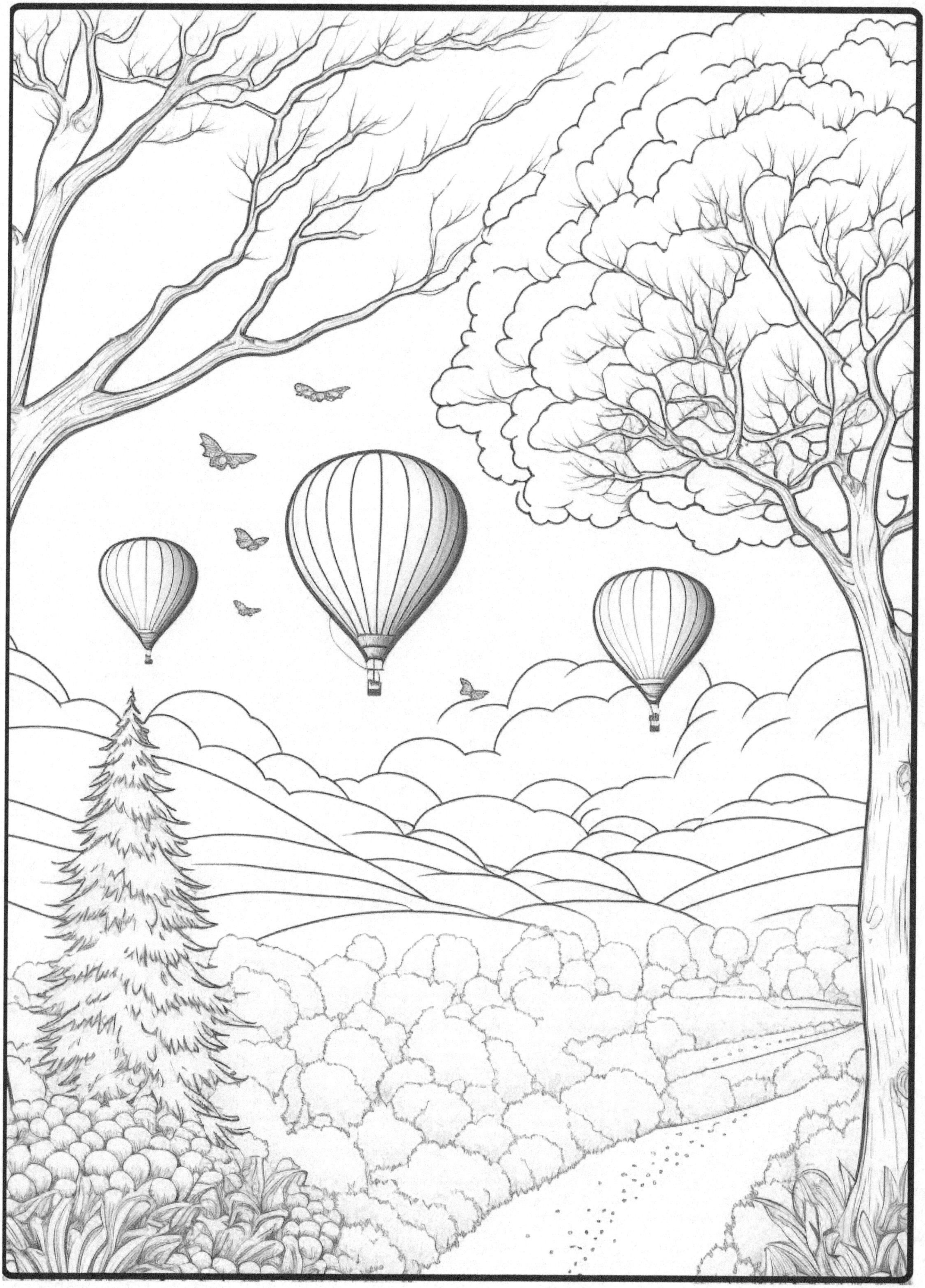

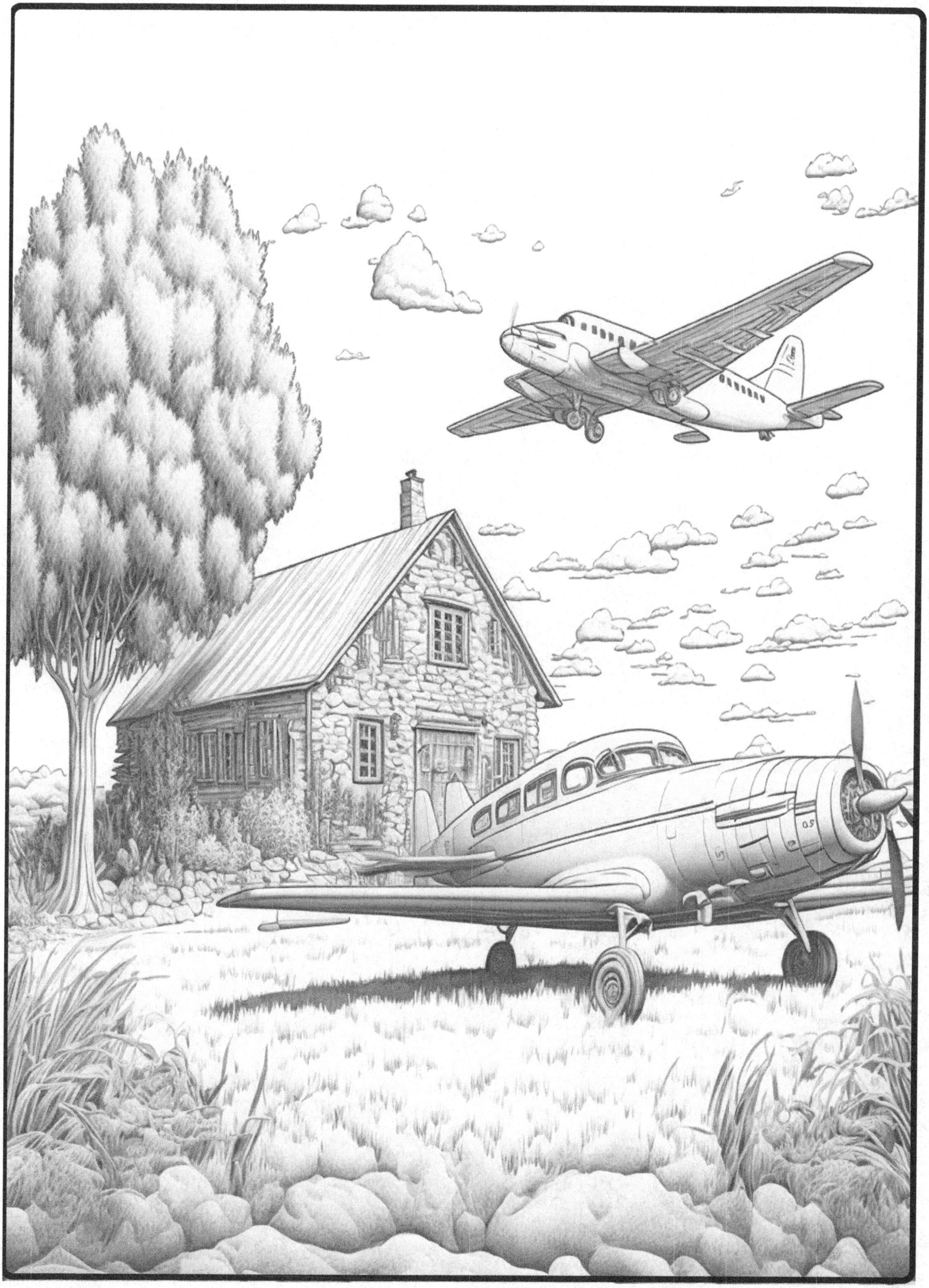

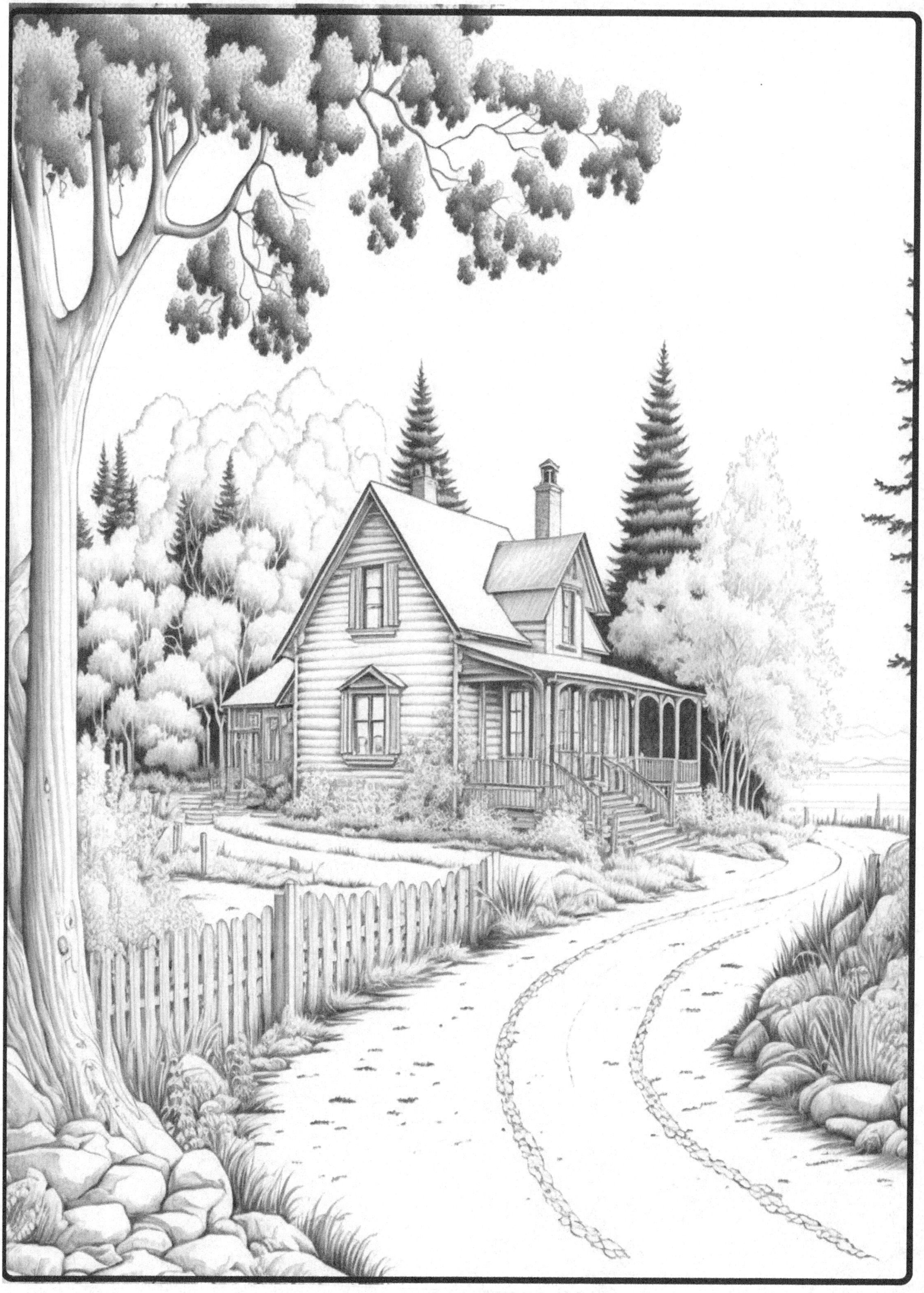

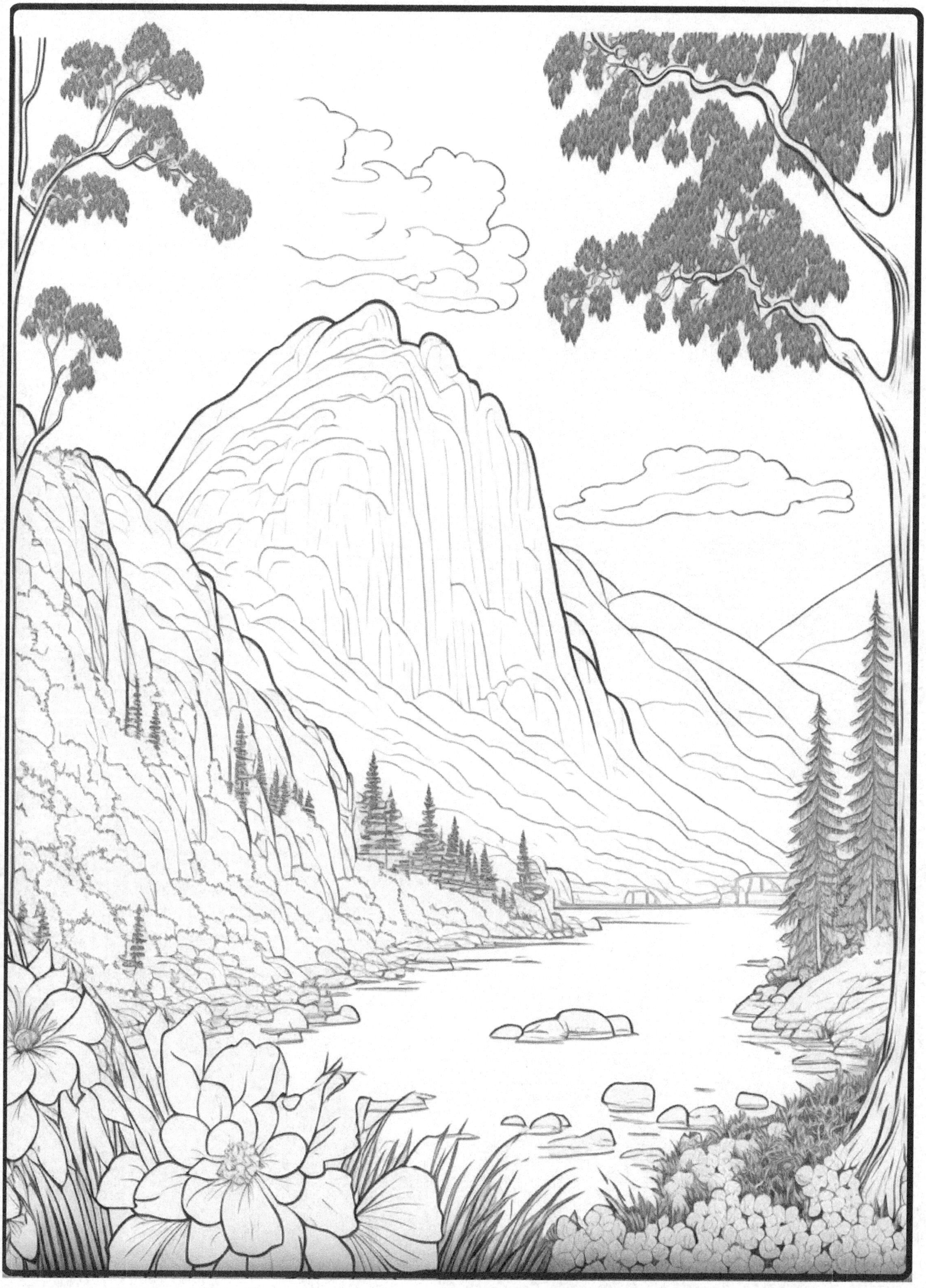

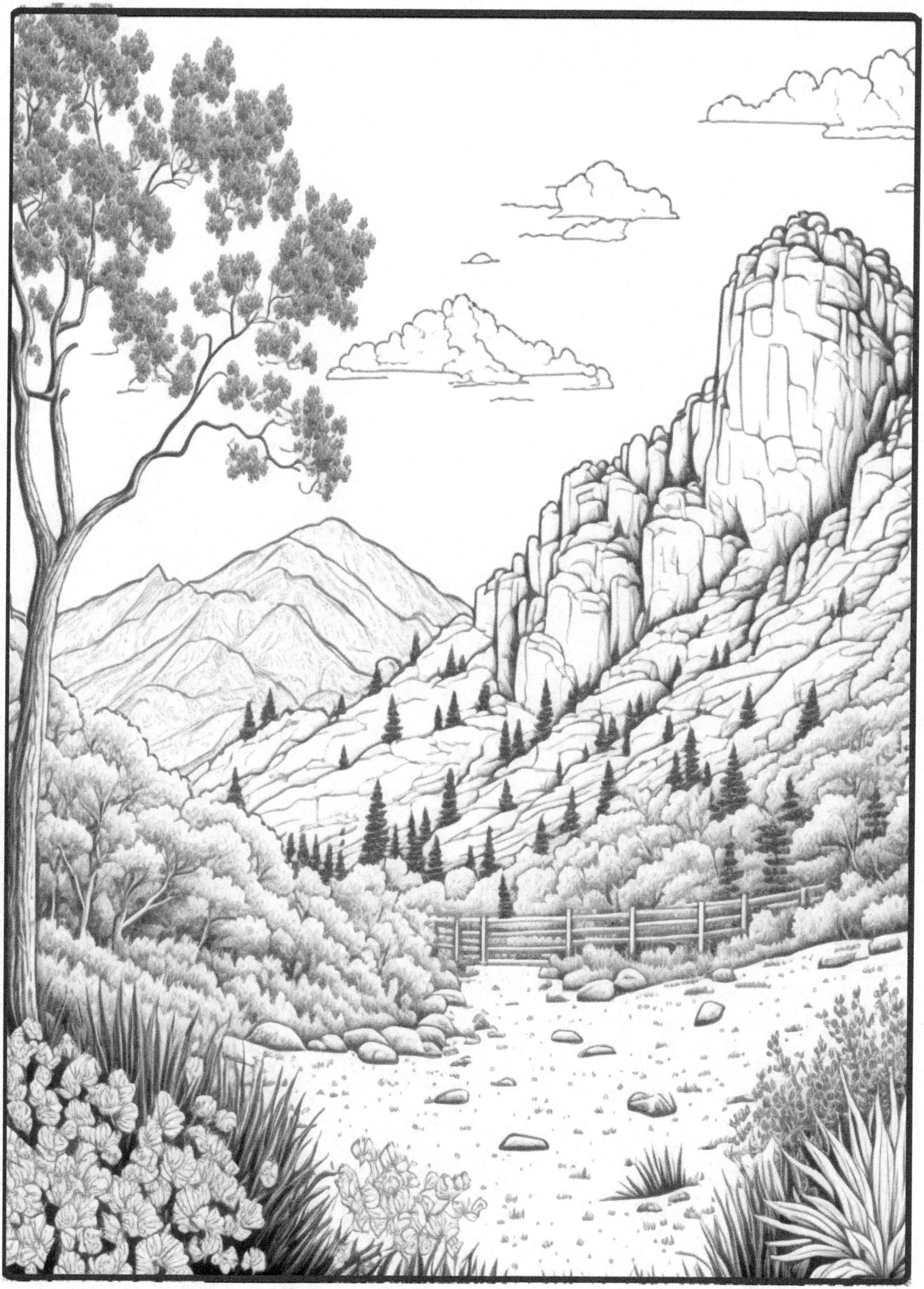

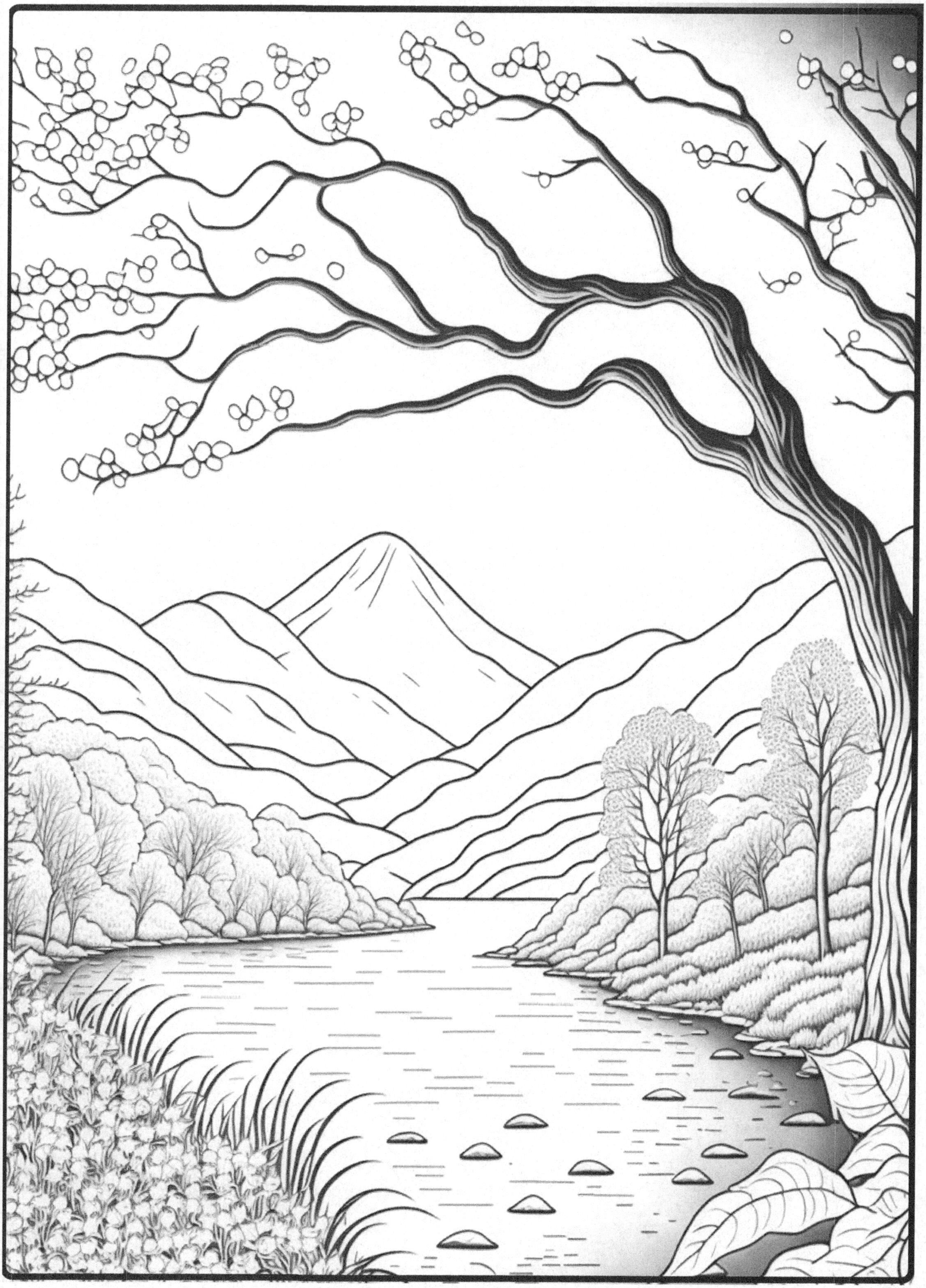

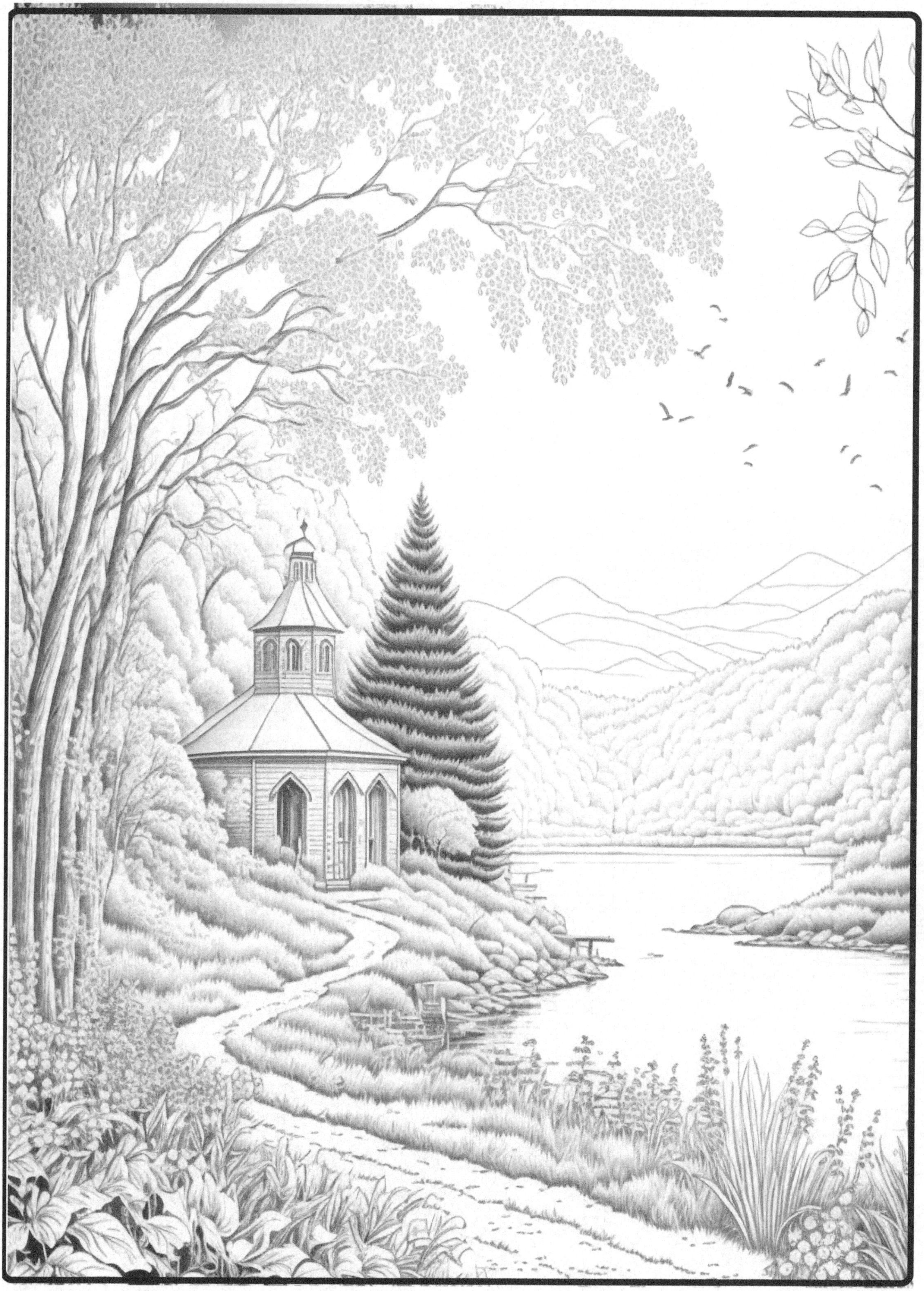

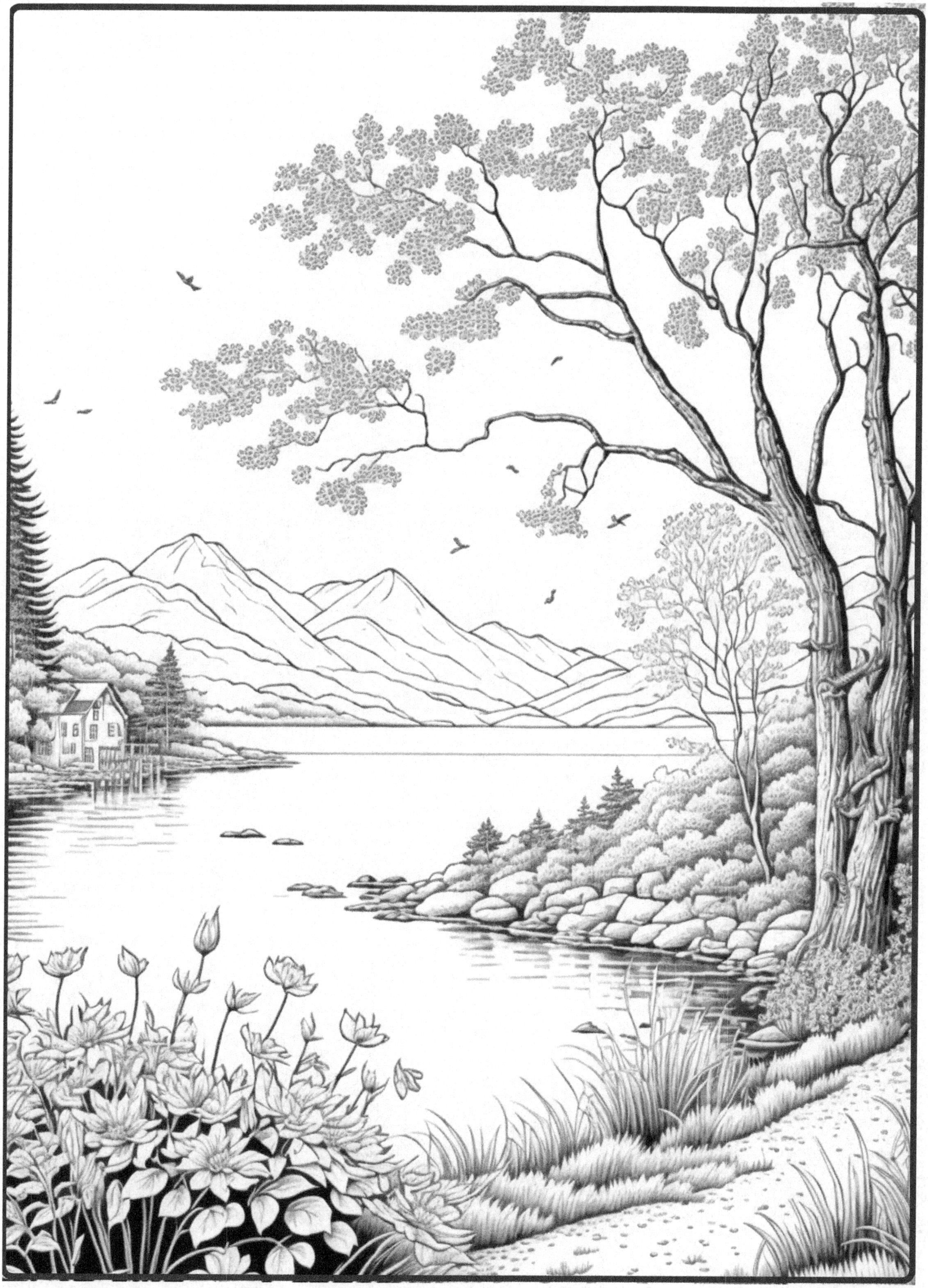

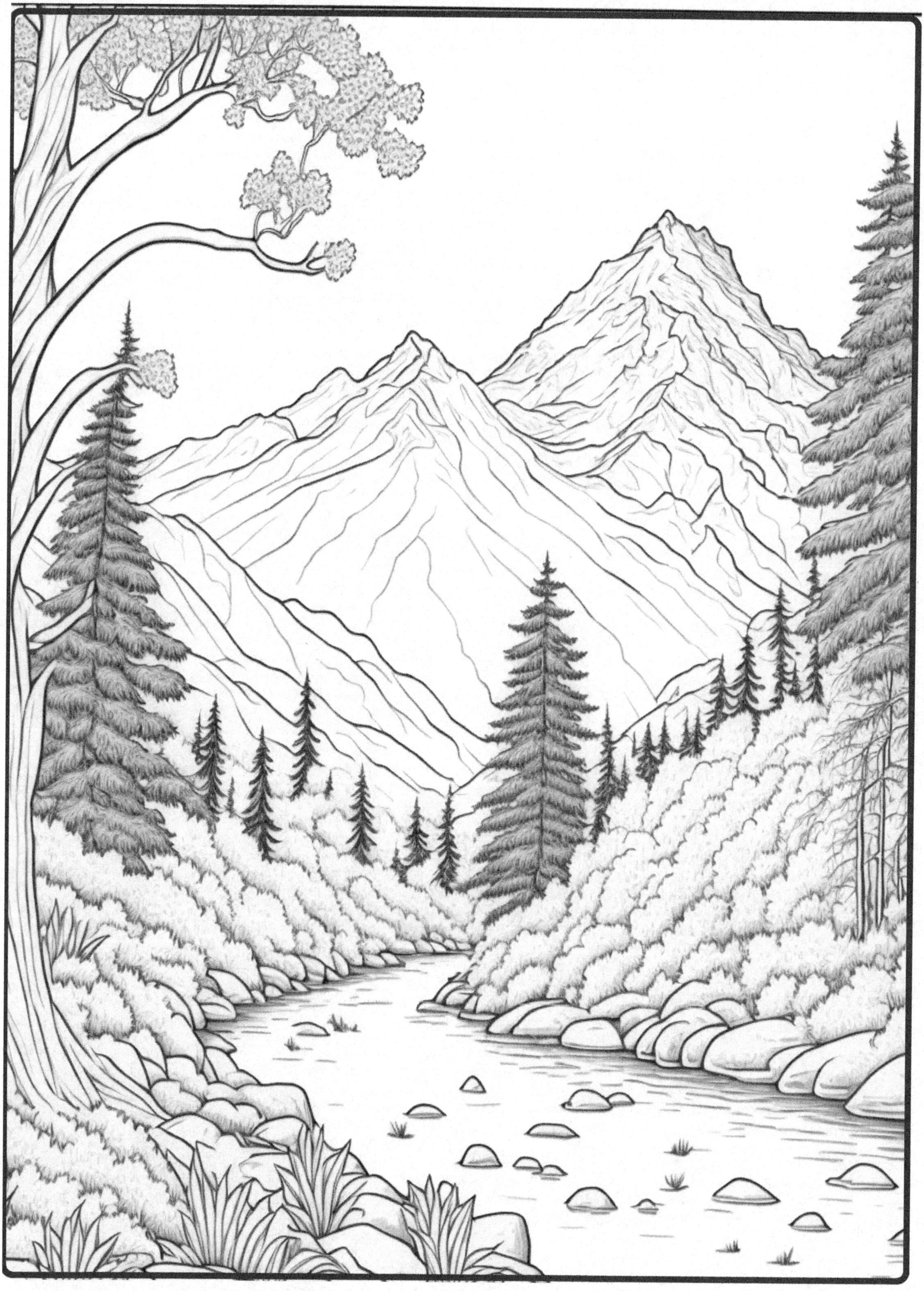

Made in the USA
Middletown, DE
10 October 2023

40516872R00057